CANE C[ ]

AND
THE CANE CORSO

Your Perfect
Cane Corso Guide

Covers Cane Corso, Cane Corso Puppies, Cane Corso Training, Cane Corso Breeders, Cane Corso Size, Health, & More!

Mark Manfield

© DYM Worldwide Publishers

DYM Worldwide Publishers

ISBN: 978-1-911355-58-8

3

will not be liable for, the websites being temporary or being removed from the Internet. The accuracy and completeness of the information provided herein, and opinions stated herein are not guaranteed or warranted to produce any particular results, and the advice or strategies, contained herein may not be suitable for every individual. The author, publisher, distributors, and/or affiliates shall not be liable for any loss incurred as a consequence of the use and application, directly or indirectly of any information presented in this work. This publication is designed to provide information regarding the subject matter covered. The information included in this book has been compiled to give an overview of the topics covered. The information contained in this book has been compiled to provide an overview of the subject. It is not intended as medical advice and should not be construed as such. For a firm diagnosis of any medical conditions, you should consult a doctor or veterinarian (as related to animal health). The writer, publisher, distributors, and/or affiliates of this work are not responsible for any damages or negative consequences following any of the treatments or methods highlighted in this book. Website links are for informational purposes only and should not be seen as a personal endorsement; the same applies to any products or services mentioned in this work. The reader should also be aware that although the web links included were correct at the time of writing they may become out of date in the future. Any pricing or currency exchange rate information was accurate at the time of writing but may become out of date in the future. The Author, Publisher, distributors, and/or affiliates assume no responsibility for pricing and currency exchange rates mentioned within this work.

Table of Contents

Introduction
to the Cane Corso

If you're thinking of raising a Cane Corso (*pronounced as "Kah-Naye Kor-so"*), then you can look forward to having a special relationship with one of the most imposing breeds of dogs. It has a strong musculature that is regal and telling of its potentials. When properly trained, it can be a very able protector, guardian, hunter, and work dog.

Cane Corsos are keen and intelligent animals, and as an experienced owner, having them around is always a rewarding experience.

The Cane Corso, otherwise known as the Italian Mastiff, was originally bred in Italy. Its legacy stretches back to ancient times, to the realm of ancient Roman conquerors, battlefields, and farmlands. True to its alternative name, this breed has the look of a mastiff. Its large head is its most prominent feature. It also has floppy ears hanging just below the eyes, which can be cropped for a more proud and standoffish look.

As with deciding any purchase that requires a long-term commitment, you must take into consideration certain aspects like your living arrangements and expenses, as well as your personality and needs, to know if a Cane Corso is the best kind of breed for you to raise.

It takes a special kind of owner to meet a Cane Corso's needs. Indeed, the Cane Corso is not for the weak of heart. This breed can be quite dominant and has a strong sense of hierarchy. It has a rambunctious nature that can potentially wreak havoc in your surroundings. That's why you need to have a firm grip and control, and exude intelligence and self-confidence, for this breed to reach its fullest potential. And if you do your best, you will have a companion that displays nearly human-like qualities.

With its bulk, size, and power, it has been known as a protector of the family. Through responsible care, Cane Corsos grow up to be gentle giants that are extremely loyal to their owners. The breed has even been known to save family members in times of peril.

It is not unusual to hear of Cane Corsos doing heroic acts. As a matter of fact, the Cane Corso ranks 7th among all dog breeds when it comes to saving lives. Apart from this, the breed has an affectionate side for children. But unlike other breeds, they tend to be quite shy around kids; they give them a lot of space, only overseeing them from afar with a protective concern. With a Cane Corso around, you know the kids will be in good hands.

This breed is also a great companion for whatever activity you have because of its dual personality. Not only can they keep up with all your outdoor activities, but they can also tame themselves when you need silence and contemplation.

Cane Corsos are keen and intelligent animals, and as an experienced owner, having them around is always a rewarding experience. They are very trainable—they can easily try new activities and can be taught many tricks. They even outdo other mastiffs when it comes to athleticism, agility, speed, and sense of adventure.

So, are you now excited to raise a Cane Corso? This book will help you delve deeper into the standards and specifications of this breed. You will also get a historical look at the breed's lineage and amazing comeback in the modern world, for you to further appreciate its nature and personality. Furthermore, you will be able to pick up valuable information on diet, nutrition, and supplies, and even ways to find a reputable breeder!

There will also be comparisons with other breeds, and a tell-all of the benefits and pitfalls of owning a Cane Corso—everything to help you become the proud owner of a breed that has one of the most enduring legacies in the world.

CHAPTER 1

Cane Corso History: How Did the Breed Emerge?

T he Mastiff refers to a group of giant dogs with various breed types, supposedly originating from Asia. Ancient Chinese references show of the existence of Mastiffs way back in 1121 B.C. The existence of Mastiffs in Egypt in 3000 B.C. was also established with the discovery of hieroglyphics of Mastiff-like dogs.

The Cane Corso is a type of Mastiff and typically shares the characteristics and history of this type.

However, today's Mastiff breed has roots from the Old English Mastiff, which were bred in England and were originally employed by their masters to fight off wolves and to guard property from ancient times.

Quite significantly, the Mastiffs caught Julius Caesar's attention in 55 B.C. during his invasion of Britain. He described the dogs as having fought bravely beside their English owners.

When the Romans brought these British dogs back home, they were used for other purposes. They became objects of public combat, particularly in the gladiator arena, to fight bulls, bears, lions, tigers, and even human gladiators! Although dog fighting has been outlawed in the modern era, it continues as an underground spectacle to date and until two centuries ago was quite legal and considered a "gentleman's sport."

The Cane Corso and the Ancient Canis Pugnax (Ancient Roman Dog): How the Cane Corso is also known as the Roman Cane Corso

The Cane Corso has a history that dates back to ancient Roman times. It has roots from the Roman war dog of the first century called the Canis Pugnax. During that period, the Cane Corso fought in ancient Roman battlefields together with legionaries of the Roman Empire. It served as a shield and protector of the warriors on the battlefield. Also, it has a reputation as a tenacious fighter in the gladiator arena, fighting humans, lions, tigers and other animals of the wild.

The Romans were not the first to use war dogs, but their militaristic minds guaranteed using the dog to its full effect. The ancient Cane Corsos wore spiked collars around their ankles and necks, adding to their fearsome visage. To fuel their ferocity, the dogs were often half-starved before unleashing them in battle towards an unsuspecting enemy. Ultimately, the Cane Corso was integral to the Roman battlefield and considered as an "auxiliary warrior."

But when the Roman Empire saw its fall, the Cane Corso found a new purpose. It was realized that it could be just as at home in the pastoral setting, as it was on the battlefield. The Cane Corso became a reputable companion, protector, and work dog for the Italians. The breed was used as a cattle driver, carrying heavy animals to the market or slaughterhouses. It also protected properties against thieves and animal predators.

In those times in the countryside, the Cane Corso was often chained to guard the stabled livestock, only allowing it a certain free range of motion. This was to protect bystanders and passersby and to keep confrontational dogs apart. After all, the Cane Corso still preserved its vicious war dog nature. The collar of the Cane Corso was often decorated with the family coat of arms. The breed was also often seen traveling alongside carts and stagecoaches, protecting the owners and contents from thieves and other attackers. With its instinct to protect, the Cane Corso earned the name Cohors, which means Guardian or Protector in Latin.

The Cane Corso was also used as a flock guardian to drive wolves away. It was equipped with a special collar to give it an advantage over wolves. Aside from that, the Cane Corso had a role in keeping animals under control, particularly in the breeding of swine. When a sow hides in a thicket to protect its young, the Cane Corso sniffs out the location, then gradually attacks and incapacitates it by biting its ear or snout. Then at the signal of the farmer, the dog releases the sow so the farmer can safely gather the litter.

Furthermore, the Cane Corso was indispensable for hunting wild boars, which were then endemic to the Italian countryside. When the boar began to attack with its dangerous tusks, the danger was very real. The Cane Corso, ever vigilant, would leap to the rescue of its master when this happened.

Back then, wild boars were also an important food source, along with badgers and porcupines, which are all native to the Italian countryside. Cane Corsos were often organized in packs to specifically hunt these wild animals.

World War II: What Led to the Cane Corso's Decline?

The idyllic life of the Cane Corso in the countryside eventually saw a decline. In the 1800s, otherwise known as the Industrial Revolution, farms began turning to modern methods of machinery, which displaced most of the Cane Corso's work. That time also saw a rise in the use of firearms, which meant new ways of hunting, and further diminishing the usefulness of the Cane Corso.

Later, during the 1970's, the existence of the Cane Corso diminished and could only be found in a few areas in Southernmost Italy.

Onwards to World War I, the decline of the Cane Corso continued. With the onset of the war much of the populous south, which relied on agricultural activity, was called to arms. A period of stability after the war was also short-lived, as World War II erupted only a few years later.

The age of war meant a decline in rural activities, and the Cane Corso became only an afterthought. There was disarray in the provinces, which was mainly left to women and children, while the men supported industry in the cities. Poverty was rife, so food rationing was strictly imposed. When the men returned after the war, they completely abandoned the fields, choosing other work opportunities in more urbanized areas.

How They Were Revived: The Incredible Work of Dr. Breber

During the 1970's, the existence of the Cane Corso diminished and could only be found in the farthest hinterlands of Southern Italy. The breed found its way to survive in the remote backwoods, under the care of farmers who stuck to an archaic system of farming. These peasants kept and trained the dog in traditional ways. However, the number of Cane Corsos left at the time was dwindling.

1976 was a turning point for the Cane Corso as it ushered its revival. Dr. Paolo Breber published an article on the Italian Kennel Club about the Cane Corso, which started to revive its image in the public imagination.

Two years before that, Dr. Breber was trying to resuscitate the breed. He acquired a few specimens of the Cane Corso, which he sent to the Malavasi brothers from Mantova, who were breeding German Shepherds at the time. He sent Dauno, a typical large black Cane Corso. It was bred with a dog named Tipsi, who produced the most significant lineage of Cane Corso in modern history. From this lineage, the models for the standard male and female Cane Corso were chosen.

In 1983, the chief proponents of the breed's recovery formed a breed club for the Cane Corso called the Society Amatori Cane Corso. In 1994, the Cane Corso received official recognition from the Italian Kennel Club (ENCI), which is responsible for dog pedigree registration services in Italy. By 1996, the breed also received recognition from the World Canine Organization (FCI).

What is the Modern Cane Corso?

Cane Corso enthusiasts formed the Società Amatori Cane Corso (SACC) in 1983. It was organized to rescue the race and establish the finer points of the Cane Corso. They found the need to differentiate the Cane Corso from other Italian Molosso hounds, specifically the Neapolitan Mastiff.

There came a renewed enthusiasm for the Cane Corso, and that resulted in the unrestrained production of litters. While that may be a good thing for sheer numbers, considering that the breed was previously almost extinct, the production *en masse* favored quantity over quality. This kept the breed from being recognized at the international level.

With a goal to maintain the eminence of the Cane Corso, the best specimens were gathered at Arese in 1996, to determine the exact characteristics the breed must have. A dog named Boris was used as the model for the perfect Cane Corso qualities. From there, the breeding strategies were improved, and finally, after a few months during the same year, the Cane Corso was recognized by the World Canine Organization.

What is the Giant Cane Corso or King Corso?

You might have heard the name somewhere. Don't get confused, though. The Giant Cane Corso or King Corso is just another name for the Cane Corso.

Similarly, Cane Corsos also go by the name *Cane da Corso*, which is basically what the breed is called back in Italy.

CHAPTER 2

What Modern Role Does the Cane Corso Fulfill?

T he Cane Corso has proven its usefulness through the centuries. Its power, stability, and intelligence have been tested on battlefields and farmlands. Today, the Cane Corso can be adapted to modern use in a variety of settings

Cane Corsos have proven to be very efficient "catch dogs."

Cane Corso as a Coursing Mastiff

The Cane Corso is considered to be the last "Coursing Mastiff." It exceeds other mastiffs regarding speed, athleticism, agility, and energy level, that's why it's the only breed that can participate in coursing.

Coursing is a hunting technique practiced way back in time by the nobility, the landed, and the wealthy. It involves dogs chasing other animals (typically a hare, a rabbit, a fox or a deer). The dogs must catch their prey through force of speed and sight, not by scent.

Cane Corso as a Catch Dog

Cane Corsos have proven to be very efficient "catch dogs." Catch dogs are specially-trained dogs that help in hunting large animals, working livestock, and baiting. Catch dogs are often outfitted with chest armor to prevent them from being pierced by their chaser, such as a boar's tusks. Cane Corsos use their teeth and weight to immobilize the animal. It can work in tandem with the farmer who often does the duty of hog-tying the prey.

Meanwhile, when it comes to boar hunting, the Cane Corso takes hold of the base of the boar's ears. Once the boar is subdued, the dog will immobilize it for as long as he can, or until the handlers arrive to dispatch the boar.

Cane Corso as a Hunting Dog

In hunting, the dog is required to chase, retrieve, and sometimes kill the game. With its versatile abilities, the Cane Corso is a perfect option for hunting.

Cane Corso as a Guard Dog

A guard dog is employed to monitor a property against thieves, unwanted people, or animals. The dog is trained to discriminate between familiar people and unfamiliar ones. The guard dog uses barking as a way to initially stave off the intruder. It also has the further capacity to attack or restrain. In this capacity, Cane Corsos, with their natural discernment and size, make perfect guard dogs.

Cane Corso as a Working Dog

As it was in the beginning, Cane Corsos still prove to be great companions in working, especially in the farmlands. It can drive livestock in the pastures. Their strength is also handy when it comes to cattle driving.

The Cane Corso's temperament is said to be agreeable to livestock. It doesn't bite or harass farm animals. When a livestock animal gives birth, even in the absence of its master, the Cane Corso will never harm the offspring. This is an example of the dual nature of the breed's assertiveness and intelligent discernment.

Cane Corso as a Police Dog

Dogs have been integrated deeply into human societies because of their loyalty and trustworthiness. No wonder they come in to help in the roles of human beings, even in saving lives and solving crimes. Of course, we are referring to police dogs.

These dogs are trained to track and immobilize possible criminals. They assist officers in making arrests and investing the scene of a crime. They are trained to sniff out illegal materials and perform search and rescue operations. It takes versatility to become a police dog! One of the most outstanding breeds perfect in this field of work is the Cane Corso.

CHAPTER 3

Can You Handle a Cane Corso? A Review

Every dog has a unique personality, and bringing one to your home is always an exciting and novel experience. Imagine having a friend and companion that will be there for life. Cane Corsos, being naturally-protective guard dogs, are a welcome addition to any home.

Cane Corsos, being naturally-protective yet loyal, are a great addition to the right home.

However, it should be noted that owners have unique needs and personalities as well. Would yours be a good fit for a Cane Corso? More importantly, will your living conditions allow you to keep and raise a Cane Corso? We will venture further in getting to know this breed regarding its inner qualities and its needs.

Qualities of a Cane Corso to Help You Decide if It's Right for You to Raise One

1. **The Cane Corso is big.** It is important to know that the Cane Corso is a medium to large-sized dog. A fully-grown Cane Corso can weigh up to 110 pounds (49kg). Don't just be caught up by appearances because they can be misleading. Yes, Cane Corsos look smart and regal, and you would certainly look like a superstar walking with your handsome companion. But again, consider that they grow to be big dogs, so imagine handling all that energy and power each day.

2. **The Cane Corso is very energetic.** Coupled with their size, Cane Corsos are hefty balls of energy. They are the most adventurous, energetic, and athletic of the Mastiffs. While that may be a good thing, oftentimes, if they are left unmanaged, their energy and enthusiasm can also lead to collateral damage. We're talking broken windows, torn carpets, plowed sofas! You may need a lot of patience (and a lot of budget for restoration fees) to keep up with a pet like this.

3. **The Cane Corso is serious, protective, and sensitive.** Because they have that domineering instinct, they may not get along with everyone instantly. They have a reputation for fighting off people and dogs they are not familiar with.

   Even when trained, a Cane Corso can still have its moments of unrestrained temperament. Because it is historically a guard dog, it will always tend to be aggressive and protective, no matter how much you train it otherwise. It will always fight back when provoked. It will repel even your friends who come by to visit you in your house because it's a place that a Cane Corso considers as a territory. In any case, its instinct to protect its pack, who happens to be you and your family, will always prevail. Because of this, be aware that the Cane Corso should be supervised and socialized early and often to reduce the likelihood of any undue aggression.

But looking on the flipside of these qualities, the Cane Corso is extremely loyal, and will go the extra mile to protect and save you if you need it!

Also, understand that a dog will go through behavioral changes, depending on how it was handled. It will outgrow its cute puppy stage, and it may grow to have some detrimental behaviors if not handled with proper leadership and training.

4. **The Cane Corso likes being active.** Cane Corsos, like any true working dog, need to be engaged in regular physical activity. You can't have your Cane Corso hanging out and about, doing nothing all day long. Its history has made it eager to have duties, and that hasn't changed in modern times. It needs constant mental stimulation, regular training, and exercise. If Cane Corsos don't work both physically and mentally, they will degenerate, fall into mischief, and will end up not using their capacities as they should to be healthy and fulfilled.

Strenuous activities are also needed for them to maintain the condition of their key organs like the heart and lungs. Just like their human companions, they need to keep moving to develop and tone their muscles. You must take an adult Cane Corso on a jog of a mile or more in the morning, and if possible, another mile during the evening. As for the young ones, they can make do with shorter walks but make it more than once a day.

However, more than just the exercise, you need to let your Cane Corso work, as this has always been its nature from the very beginning. This could be a good thing—whatever job you may want help with, the Cane Corso will be there to deliver.

5. **The Cane Corso can't be left to run freely.** An obedience-trained Cane Corso can enjoy limited and controlled off-the-leash moments. That being said, no dog is still ever safe to roam around without supervision. This is true, whether you live in the city or the countryside. Or else, that freedom may eventually have a price—the gravest of which is injury and death. Some expected results of your dog roaming around freely can also include fights with other dogs, automobile accidents, getting your dog pounded by an angry human, and irate neighbors.

6. **The Cane Corso cannot be left alone for long periods of time.** Because it always needs to be preoccupied with something, the Cane Corso cannot be left alone for extended periods. Becoming idle develops in them problematic habits like fighting with another dog, constant barking and howling, digging holes, chewing on anything they set their eyes upon, and jumping around nonstop. Sometimes, they even become violent. It all stems from the need for companionship

and energy release. Thankfully, this is easily preventable by providing proper companionship.

7. **The Cane Corso is a thinking dog.** Always remember that Cane Corsos are thinking dogs. For a trainer, it truly is a pleasure to be working with a Cane Corso, who dominates in activities that require agility, strength, and obedience. Cane Corsos love taking part in dog sports. They have a strong motivation to please, and they respond well to positive reinforcement.

8. **The Cane Corso needs to be trained.** For a Cane Corso to be at its top game, it obviously needs to be trained. A hefty hundred plus pound dog can only be a headache if you are not going to teach it important skills. This may require you to go to an obedience trainer a few times a week and invest a few minutes of sessions per day. Once you set up your role as the master of a Cane Corso, teaching skills become quite easy. Some of the skills you can easily teach a Cane Corso include lying down, staying put, or walking by your side.

But if there's one most important thing you must instill in a Cane Corso, it's obedience. Again, this breed is very unfriendly towards strangers, so you must first earn its trust. When you do earn it, its obedience will naturally follow.

Also, you need to be able to establish your household rules to a Cane Corso. You should set boundaries and make them clear early on. This is not only for it to be aware of its limitations, but also to be informed of what it needs to protect. Enforce the commands appropriately and consistently when the need arises. You need to be assertive all the time, to set expectations early and often that you are the master.

Of course, in training a Cane Corso, you don't need to have the personality of a drill sergeant. Just be assertive, be consistent with the boundaries you set, don't be fooled by the antics, and eventually, your dog will recognize you as the real leader.

9. **The Cane Corso likes to dominate.** So, what happens if you're not able to earn the obedience of a Cane Corso? A Cane Corso, much like any other breed, thinks differently—it has social hierarchies that it instinctively needs to impose in all scenarios. If you don't make it apparent that you are the boss, and you just give in to all its howling tantrums or sad looks, then it's never going to be the ideal relationship you want. Sure, they can appear to be generous and affectionate towards their so-called subordinates. Still, at the end of the day, if they don't feel like listening to you, they won't.

   When a Cane Corso feels dominant, it will try to make its own rules and implement it on others by being physical. You'll notice it assuming a dominant posture and intense stare. Sometimes, it will also make a menacing snarl and knock down anyone with a blow or a bite; but again, you can prevent this simply by being firm and consistent from the beginning!

10. **The Cane Corso needs to be docked and cropped.** In its natural state, a Cane Corso has floppy ears and a long tail. Docking and cropping are the procedures of reducing the tail and ears.

    Despite what is widespread in the media, procedures like docking and cropping are less stressful at a young age than when fully grown. These procedures are also for the health—adult dogs get an infection from whacking their large and heavy tails against walls.

Some people would say they don't want a cropped dog because the naturally floppy ears give the dog a softer expression. But this is counterintuitive; the Cane Corso is not a soft breed. Ear cropping makes the Cane Corso look standoffish, which is a good thing.

With an intimidating look, people would be more hesitant to approach the dog, rather than petting and overwhelming it head-on. The Cane Corso is very aloof with new people. It needs a few moments to assess whether a person is a threat or not. Most often, it needs a stranger to be properly introduced by the master. So, cropping is a way to protect bystanders as well, to natively recognize the power of this breed. It is of course up to you, if you'd prefer to have your Cane Corso cropped and docked, but it is recommended for the reasons mentioned.

Most responsible breeders will offer to have the procedure done before you take your pup home. The aftercare for Cane Corso cropping is also very easy and painless. Because it is done during its 7th to 12th week, there is very little posting of the ears (securing them temporarily to help them set into a certain position), like you would see in Great Danes or Dobermans.

11. **The Cane Corso needs to be integrated into your house and life.** Having a Cane Corso means adding a new member to the family. While it may appear indifferent to strangers, this breed thrives on companionship and love from its master. That means it will want to sleep, eat, and do just about anything besides you. So, consider your responsibilities—if you have a job or other obligations that need your full focused attention and time, then a Cane Corso might not be for you.

This breed drools a lot, especially when eating and drinking water!

The Cane Corso does manage being left at home from time to time, but it still shouldn't be stuck chained or locked in the back yard, especially when it can see the whole family interacting inside the house. You can make your Cane Corso work all you want—in fact, its delight is to see you being unburdened of some tasks. But if you make it feel that it doesn't have any use at home, and worse, if it doesn't feel it has a place in the family, then it will start showing acts of rebellion.

12. **The Cane Corso is messy.** This breed drools a lot, especially when eating and drinking water. There is no solution for this; all you can do is place a towel or protective mat underneath the eating and drinking area. Also, while it does not grow long coats of hair, the Cane Corso does shed. So that means it needs professional grooming too, at least twice a year. You

need to also be prepared for the dog's coat blowing, a seasonal occurrence in breeds with a double coat. You may see dust-like hair begin to float around your house. So, you may want to consider this if you have allergies. A good way to test this is if possible, spend time with a friend or breeder's Cane Corso, to see if you have allergic symptoms. Better to find out earlier rather than later if you are prone to allergies from your potential new friend!

Despite the Cane Corso being a bit messy, this doesn't mean that you must be a person who is tolerant of an ongoing mess. What this implies is you should be a person who values a dog's company more than the neatness of your home. You have to deal with a slightly messy house, and this is true for all dogs. Dogs are like children; they create a mess from time to time. They can't help it, but a small dose of tolerance (along with a good shot of boundary setting), will lead to a happy coexistence!

13. **The Cane Corso needs maintenance.** A Cane Corso needs a fair amount of maintenance. You will have to invest a good amount, to be able to sustain its food properly, and ensure its health care needs.

   As a large dog, it follows that it will require large servings at meal times. This also translates to its waist being more sizeable than average. In addition to this, it can also cost you more bills at the veterinary clinic. For one, the medications it must take should be proportionate to its body weight. Also, spaying or neutering, a prerequisite for any dog, can be more expensive because of the Cane Corso's size. Cane Corsos are also prone to hip dysplasia, which can be costly for your budget.

The annual outlays for immunizations and local licensing are the same for all breeds. But to reiterate, all dogs need a fair amount of upkeep, and it will not be inexpensive no matter how cheaply the dog was acquired.

Basic obedience training classes are also a must for any Cane Corso, especially if you are a first-time owner.

Be sure to make arrangements in your will or with your family so that it can continue to receive proper care, in the event you predecease your dog. Many owners fail to do that, that's why many pets are also left feeling abandoned and miserable in the remaining years of their life.

14. **Breeding the perfect Cane Corso is expensive.** The initial cost of having a Cane Corso is quite costly. The breeding program for your Cane Corso is expensive because you need to take into consideration factors like temperament, trainability, and physical soundness, for it to be successful. You can always go for the alternative, which is getting your dog from a less credible breeder. However, these small-time breeders sometimes unselectively mate any two Cane Corsos of the opposite sex, and this can produce unforeseen issues. In the long run, this can also require from you a hefty price, because your dog will most likely suffer from bad health, an extreme temperament, and lack of socialization in the lineage.

Of course, there is also the option of getting an adult or older pup from the shelter or another owner. While you may not have witnessed firsthand the birth of these Cane Corsos, and in some cases, these dogs even come from the horrifying experience of being abandoned, they still have the potential to be marvelous dogs if they are given the right training, as well as enough amount of love and understanding.

What are the Benefits of Getting a Cane Corso?

While there may be challenges to getting a Cane Corso, there are also more benefits that make raising it a rewarding experience.

A Cane Corso's appearance is a foremost advantage. Due to its size, a Cane Corso can make a formidable guard dog and protector. It is also full of energy, spirit, and athleticism and can be trained for many tasks. It can't be repeated often enough: the Cane Corso is a working dog. If you are an experienced dog owner who wants to venture into another challenge, a Cane Corso and its unique attributes may just be for you.

Cane Corsos are among the smartest and most trainable breeds. It is a highly intelligent dog, so it can absorb a lot of information. It likes overwhelming tasks because it needs constant mental stimulation.

With a Cane Corso, you have an intelligent dog that can be employed in various capacities. It can help you with tasks like opening and closing doors, fetching something you need, and picking up toys. It is always thinking about how to please its handler, so it will dutifully do whatever is required with a bit of initial encouragement.

From the very beginning, a Cane Corso was employed in the capacity of a guard dog and work dog, and because of this, it has developed an assertive and confident personality. It will be very able to protect you and your family. A Cane Corso will not back down from threats. In contrast, it can also be sensitive enough to know when to be calm and quiet.

Another benefit you can get from having a Cane Corso is that it truly will feel loyalty and the desire to be with you. If you want a good companion dog, a Cane Corso is a perfect option. It wants to share many of your activities in a day; it will even want to go to work with you, if possible. Do you want an exercise buddy? Do you like trekking, hiking, and other physical activities? What about sports like Frisbee? Then look no further than the Cane Corso as your willing partner in crime!

Constant exercise is very beneficial for the overall health of a Cane Corso. An adult Cane Corso will not get exhausted from mile-long runs compared to other breeds. If you enjoy training a dog, then a Cane Corso will welcome these experiences.

Finally, a Cane Corso can live up to twelve years (and sometimes longer), and that is a fair amount of time of love, loyalty, and friendship from such a marvelous breed and friend!

How Much Space Does a Cane Corso Need?

Cane Corsos can adapt very well to living in the city, just be sure to get in some good outside time.

Historically, the Cane Corso was employed in a variety of capacities throughout Italy. It's true that space is ideally needed for a fully-grown Cane Corso since it is an active dog. However, you don't need to worry if you are not living in a large house. The Cane Corso can very well adapt to living in the city.

Of course, the space that the dog needs depends on you and your activity level. If you are an active person and can spend time with your dog several times a day, then a Cane Corso can adapt to a smaller space. It just needs to be exercised regularly each day to keep it from being bored and developing nasty habits. But if you have other responsibilities that keep you away from home for extended hours every day, and if you have not structured activity for the dog, you may need to have a bigger space for it to run and explore by itself.

Cane Corso and Your family

A Cane Corso will love your family, it just needs to feel included like anyone else. Integrating the dog into the family should be no hassle since it has a strong sense of loyalty. The breed has been employed as a guard dog, after all. It will protect the whole family because it quickly starts to see every member as part of its "pack."

If there is an impending threat to any of your family members, it will always be there to the rescue. A Cane Corso also loves joining family activities, especially physical ones. Jogging, hiking, and playing with the kids are some of the things that Cane Corso would love to do often.

Cane Corso and Your Kids: Will It Be a Good Fit?

To some, the juxtaposition of a child and a Cane Corso may be alarming because a Cane Corso is a huge, fearsome-looking dog. The concern is valid, and many people will always have this misconception regarding large animals. But then again, the Cane Corso is an intelligent breed of dog. Despite its looks, it is a very friendly dog that does very well with kids. It may be surprising, but the Cane Corso has several attributes that can help integrate well with children.

For one, the Cane Corso has a high pain tolerance. Kids are very rambunctious and may unintentionally hurt a dog. Other dogs would be more reactive to pain and may act in defense, but a Cane Corso's makeup is different. Children's rough behavior will not hurt this dog.

Additionally, the Cane Corso can adapt well to a new family member. It can interact with people it considers being non-threatening. It is a very loving dog, not just a playmate. It has a very nurturing side. You may often find a Cane Corso acting as a 'parent' figure for a child. It will act like this to make sure that the child is safe and well-behaved.

However, although Cane Corsos are calm despite being large dogs, some precautions should still be taken. There are times when a Cane Corso may accidentally knock over a very small child, so always be there to supervise your children when around the dog. Remember that you cannot leave young children and babies alone with dogs, whether it's a big or small one.

As for your kids who are big enough, teach them certain responsibilities in handling dogs. Remind them to give the dog respect, space, and fairness. Cane Corsos respond well to training and commands. If your children are old enough to give instructions themselves, you may be ready for a Cane Corso. Overall, a Cane Corso's temperament is a good fit for children because of its protective and sensitive nature.

CHAPTER 4

What are the Cane Corso Standards and Colors? What To Look for in a Cane Corso

T he Neapolitan Mastiff, like the Cane Corso, is a Molosser type of dog. It is good to distinguish the two because of their similar origins and monikers. Like the Cane Corso, the Neapolitan Mastiff was nearly extinct during the World Wars. The Neopolitan Mastiff breed was revived by Italian painter Piero Scianzani. Both breeds originated in Italy.

The Cane Corso is playful, but even they get tired sometimes!

Neapolitan Mastiff (Mastino Napoletano) and the Cane Corso

Primarily the Neapolitan Mastiff is a protector or guard of the family. The Cane Corso was employed in the fields where it served varied roles as a guardian dog, herd dog, and hunter.

There are some very distinct differences between a Neapolitan Mastiff and a Cane Corso, and it is obvious at first sight.

Appearance & Face

The Neapolitan Mastiff has a fleshier, more wrinkled appearance with loose skin hanging down its jowls. The face of the Cane Corso is broader and tauter, compared to the Neapolitan Mastiff. The Neopolitan Mastiff has a somewhat somber and sad expression, while the Cane Corso looks sharp and smart.

Weight (Build)

Neapolitan Mastiffs are heftier at around 60 kg (132 lbs) for males and 50 kg (110 lbs) for females. The Cane Corso is more lightweight and has a sturdier build, tipping the scale at around 45 kg (99 lbs) for males and 40 kg (88 lbs) for females.

Other Names

The Cane Corso is also otherwise known as Italian Mastiff, Cane Corz, and Cane de Macellaio.

The Neopolitan Mastiff is also known as the Neo, Italian Bulldog, Italian Mastiff, Mastino Napoletano, and Italian Molosso.

Color

Both dogs have similar color varieties. Neapolitan Mastiffs come in black, blue, mahogany, tawny, and brindle colors. Cane Corso colors come in fawn, black, red, gray, black brindle, blue, and chestnut brindle colors.

Life Expectancy

The Neapolitan Mastiffs have a minimum life expectancy of 8 years while the Cane Corso's is 10 years. The maximum life expectancy of Neos is ten years, and the Cane Corso is 11 years. As with people, you truly never know how long they'll live exactly, but enjoy them while they are around!

Height

The maximum height of Neapolitan Mastiffs is 30 inches (76.2 cm) for males and 28 inches (71.1 cm) for females. The maximum height of the Cane Corso is 28 inches (71.1 cm) for male and 26 inches (66 cm) for female.

Temperament

Neapolitan Mastiffs are more obedient, sometimes stubborn; they can be dominant. They are known to be protective and fearless dogs. This makes them great companions and guard dogs.

In comparison to the Neopolitan Mastiff, the Cane Corso is more cheerful, courageous, intelligent, loyal, quiet, and social. They have been adapted to a variety of uses because of these attributes.

Cane Corso Standards: Physical Characteristics to Look Out For

General Appearance

The Cane Corso is considered to have a medium to large size body. They are robust and sturdy because of the lean muscle. Nevertheless, they have an elegant look.

Important Proportions

Cane Corsos have a rectangular outline and are slightly longer than other breeds but not too tall. (Their length is 11% greater than their height). Meanwhile, the length of their head is 36% of the height at the withers (the ridge between the shoulder blades).

Behavior/Temperament

They are extremely fast, responsive, and agile and are very good at guarding properties, livestock, and family. People in the past used these dogs for herding cattle and hunting.

Head

The large head is usually molossoid (mastiff-like). They also have upper axes that are slightly convergent with the muzzle without evident wrinkles.

Skull

The zygomatic arches of the skull are broad. Its width and length should also be equal. Its front is convex and becomes flat right at the back where the forehead is. Meanwhile, the media-frontal furrow part begins at the stop, which is well marked and ends in the middle of the skull. It is also visible.

Nose

The nose is black, but some may have a gray mask nose having a very subtle difference in tone or color. The nose should be large with open nostrils. The nose is found along the same line where the nose bridge is.

Muzzle

The muzzle or the snout is strong and square. It is evidently twice shorter than the skull. Its front part is flat with parallel lateral surfaces. It should also be broad because it is long. From the side view, you will see that the muzzle is deep, while the nasal bridge is aligned properly.

Lips

The upper lips take the shape of an inverted "U" at the meeting point. From the side view, the upper lips appear to be hanging a little. Covering the lower jaw, they determine the form of the muzzle's lower part.

Jaws and Teeth

They have very large and thick jaws that are also curved. It is slightly undershot but no more than 5 mm. A level bite should tolerable and not sought after.

Cheeks

The masseter region is seen, but it is not bulging.

Eyes

Their eyes are medium-sized that are both slightly protruding. Nevertheless, they are not exaggerated. They take the shape of an ovoid. They are also set apart, almost in a sub-frontal position. The eyelids are close fitting while the color of the iris is darker than the coat color. Expression of the eyes should be attentive and eager.

Ears

It should be triangular, drooping, and medium-sized. The ears are wide set-on that is much above the cheekbone or zygomatic arches. They are also uncropped.

Neck: The neck should be strong and muscular. It should have the same length as the head.

Body

The body measures are slightly longer than the withers height. It should appear sturdy and strong, but it should not be square.

- **Withers.** (The ridge between the shoulder blades). It is pronounced and is rising above the croup.
- **Back.** They have a muscular back that is straight and firm.
- **Loin.** (The part of the body on both sides of the spine between the lowest rib and the hip bones). The loin should be short but strong.
- **Croup.** (The top line of the dog's hindquarters). It should be long, wide, and somewhat inclined.
- **Chest.** The chest is deep and well-developed.

- **Tail.** The tail is set on fairly high; and very broad at the root. When the dog is in action, it is carried high, but never erect or curled.

Forequarters

- **Shoulder.** The shoulders are muscularly long and oblique.
- **Upper Arm.** The upper arm is strong.
- **Forearm.** The forearm should be straight, and very strong.
- **Carpus.** (Wrist) It should feel elastic.
- **Metacarpus.** (Front Pastern) The area of the leg that is below the wrist (or carpus) on the front legs but above the foot). It is elastic and just slightly sloping.
- **Forefeet.** The forefeet must have a round shape, with very arched and gathered toes like a cat's foot.

Hindquarters

- **Thigh.** It is long and broad with a back line that is convex.
- **Lower thigh.** It should look and feel strong, but not plump or fleshy.
- **Stifle or knee.** It is solid and slightly angulated.
- **Hock joint.** Like the knee, it should also look slightly angulated.
- **Metatarsus or rear pastern.** (The area of the leg below the heel (hock) but above the foot.) It should appear thick, bare, and dry.
- **Hind feet.** It is somewhat less compact and less solid than its forefeet.

- **Gait and movement.** The dog should walk in long strides and have an extended trot.

Coat

- **Skin.** The skin should be fairly thick and close-fitting.
- **Hair.** The hair is short and very dense but shiny. It should have a slight undercoat and vitreous texture.
- **Colors.** Black, slate-gray, lead-gray, light-gray, light and dark fawn colors, stag red, dark wheat color, coat with stripes of different shades and tones of fawn or gray. In brindled dogs, the black or gray mask found on the muzzle should not go over the line of the eyes. There is also a small, white spot or patch on the chest, the tips of the toes, and sometimes on the nose.

Size and Weight

Withers' length

Male. 64 cm (25.1 inches) — 68 cm (26.8 inches)
Female. 60 cm (23.62 inches) — 64 cm (25.19 inches)
With a tolerance of 2 cm (.78 inches), more or less, tall.

Weight (according to dog size)

Male. 45 kg (99 lbs) — 50 kg (110 lbs).
Female. 40kg (88 lbs) — 45 kg (99 lbs).

What are Cane Corso Faults?

Any difference or departure from the standards is called a fault. Meanwhile, the seriousness of the fault should be seen in exact proportion to the severity of its effect on the dog's health and welfare, including its ability to perform its traditional work.

Minor faults

Minor faults that can be corrected through careful breeding of the next generation.

- The lateral surfaces of the muzzle are converging, or the axes of both muzzle and skull parallel or very marked converging.
- Nose has partial depigmentation.
- Instead of normal scissor bite, the dog has an undershot bite of the dog is more than 5mm.
- The tail is in a vertical position.
- Permanent unusual gait or amble when the dog is trotting.
- Oversized or undersized.
- The presence of dewclaws (a high up claw, not touching the ground).

Disqualifying faults

Disqualifying faults are breed-type faults which diminish the overall look or structure of the breed. The structural problems may keep the dog from doing the work of its breed. One such thing is temperament that deviates from the norm. Faults keep the dog from being bred.

- Aggressive or extremely shy dogs.
- Physical or behavioral abnormalities.
- Diverging skull and axes of the muzzle
- Total nasal depigmentation.
- Dogs with a Roman nose, having concave or convex nose bridge.
- Overshot bite or overshot mouth.
- Partial or complete depigmentation of palpebral fissures such as walleye or blue- flecked and strabism (crossed-eyes), or squinted.
- The dog has no tail, or the tail is too short.
- Semi-long coat with smooth or fringed hair.
- All colors that are not included in the standard list and those with large white patches.

Notes

- All male dogs should have two normal & normally descended testicles in their scrotum.
- Dogs that are clinically healthy and have the right breed conformation should be the ones that are only used for breeding dogs.

Italian Cane Corso Standard

The Italian Cane Corso Standard describes the breed as medium-big, and having a powerful and strongly-built body, but also elegant. It also has lean and long muscles. It has a unique and distinct appearance of strength, endurance, and agility.

American Cane Corso Standard: How Do They Differ from the Italian Standards?

The Italian Cane Corso Standard describes the breed as a medium–big, has a powerful and strong build but also exhibits elegance.

In 2010, the Cane Corso was awarded the AKC (American Kennel Club) recognition by the ad hoc group, the Working Group. According to the breed standard, the size, proportion, and substance of an American Cane Corso are as follows:

They are muscular and large-boned. They are also balanced and rectangular in proportion. The length from the point of the shoulder to the buttock should be 10% greater than the height of the dog. The height refers to the measurement from the highest point of the dog's shoulder to the ground. Their height should be from 25 inches (63.5 cm) to 27.5 inches (69.9 cm), while the bitches should be from 23.5 inches (59.7 cm) to 26 inches (66 cm). The weight should appear proportionate to the height.

There is no significant difference between the Italian Cane Corso Standard and the AKC standard that was in effect in 2010. Both bodies determined the attributes of the dog and had common standards for the breed.

More About Colors

Cane Corsos come in interesting colors that are a mark of their breed. It is good to follow the standards of the breed to make sure that the dog is of good breed quality. Cane Corsos have two basic coat colors which are black and fawn. They also come in an interesting shade of gray, which is often referred to as blue. This is due to a genetic pigment reduction, diluting black to blue and formentino to fawn color. Brindle, which refers to the coat coloring pattern or streaks of another color, is common to both basic coat colors. The brindling can appear in various intensities, including trigrato or full brindle, black brindle, and blue brindle as well.

The fawn color is also expressed in different colors or hues. You will see Corsi that are pale formentino, and you will be able to find those with a shade that appears red, too. A more common color is the beige that has a back coat tipped with black. Meanwhile, blue dogs have a gray nose that is darker than their coat. The rest of the dogs with different colors, their noses appear to be black. White markings or smaller white patches can also be seen in different parts of the body, such as the chest, toes, chin, and nose.

It is good to take note of the recognized colors of the Cane Corso. Some breeders may market unusual colors of the Cane Corso and describe these as "rare." These colors are not desirable in the standard, and may, in fact, be a defect in the breed and a ground for disqualification. Remember this, if you do plan to ever breed.

(Grigio Tigrato) Blue Cane Corso also Blue Coat Cane Corso

The Blue Cane Corso (so called), is a shade of gray. These include: lead-gray, slate-gray, light-gray are genetically one color – gray – with different degrees of intensity, the gray color is in fact diluted black. The blue shade also dilutes or weakens the pigmentation of the lips, eyelids, and nose. They too become gray colored.

When crossing two gray dogs, the resulting puppies will also receive the recessive gene. From two gray dogs, the resulting puppies will be of weakened colors: gray, gray brindle, fawn with a gray mask (formentino), including undesirable ones: Isabella, gray-and-tan, uniform tan, or tan brindle.

Black Cane Corso

Some Cane Corso are completely black dogs (small white marks on a throat, breast, or fingers are allowed). If there is even just one hair of fawn color on the dog, the dog isn't genetically black. Black dogs always have a well pigmented black inking of lips, eyes, and a black pigmented nose.

Frumentiono or Formentino Cane Corso

The Formentino Cane Corso is a fawn shade, which is a shade of light brownish color. The color is always marked with a gray mask.

(Tigrato) Black Brindle Cane Corso

Brindle is a coloring pattern in animals, particularly dogs, and with the Black Brindle Cane Corso, it can appear as black stripes of various widths on a red background. These can range from thin black stripes to almost black dogs with separate red speckles (such color is sometimes called black brindle), a black mask on the face and well pigmented black lips, eyelids, and a black nose.

Red Cane Corso

The Red Cane Corso is a more intense, richer shade of fawn and it appears as a deep reddish-brown. It has the same attributes as the Formentino Cane Corso, in that it has a gray mask.

Chestnut Brindle Cane Corso

The Chestnut Brindle Cane Corso is also identified as Gray Brindle. The gray is the stripe or brindle that appears in streaks on a red background of any intensity, from pale-yellow to chestnut, a gray mask on the face, a gray nose and gray lips, and eyelids.

Gray Cane Corso

The gray Cane Corso is also known as blue Cane Corso.

What are the Non-Standard Colors of the Cane Corso?

The colors are determined by the standard, but some undesirable colors do occur in the breed. It should be noted that these colors are not more preferable or more valuable. Instead they are disqualifying traits in the breed. Dogs of undesirable colors undoubtedly are still Cane Corso, showing all the breed traits and born from two pedigree parents, but such dogs must be excluded from any breeding program.

It is necessary to pay attention to the parents of these dogs because all the undesirable colors in the breed are caused by recessive genes, and the birth at least one puppy of a non-standard color means that both of his parents are carriers of these unwanted recessive genes.

White Cane Corso

The white cane Corso is a very light shade of fawn, making it appear white or cream. It is also known as wheaten or straw shade. The mask is a shade of gray. This happens because of a gene that determines the intensity of the coat color; that's why the red shade was lowered significantly to a light color. This color is not acceptable for competition, but it is acceptable for breeding due to its genetics.

Liver or Chocolate

The Liver Cane Corso must be identified with the accepted red shade in that there the absence of a gray mask. The muzzle is completely a reddish hue tipped with a purple, pink nose. However, it is known that some livers have a black mask.

Tan Color

This color is a serious fault in the Cane Corso. It is identified by spots of the red color of any intensity. They can be present in any clear color. It can appear as the following:

- Black and Tan. Black dogs with red marks, black lips, eyes, and a black nose.
- Gray and Tan. Dogs of gray color with red marks, gray lips, eyes, and a gray nose.

Fawn Cane Corso (Fawn Without a Mask)

The Cane Corso is fawn which is a shade of light yellowish-brown color. This is expressed in three ways in the Cane Corso. There is a distinct absence of a mask which is a disqualifying attribute.

- Dogs of a fawn color without a mask, with black lips, eyes, and a black nose.
- Dogs of a fawn color, without a mask, with brown pigmentation on lips, eyes and a brown nose.
- Dogs of a fawn color, without a mask, with gray lips, eyes and a gray nose.

Isabella or Tawny

The color is diluted from the liver shade and appears grayish-yellow. Attributes of this color can include purple-pink nose and mucous membranes, a black mask, and light green-yellow hazel eyes. These colors also exist in brindle. The shade is a disqualifying fault in the breed.

Cane Corso Blue Eyes?

Cane Corso puppies usually have blue eyes, especially the blue Cane Corsos. However, as they mature, the color will change depending on the coat. Blue eyes are a disqualifying trait, according to American Cane Corso standards. The ideal eye color of a Cane Corso is a deep dark color.

CHAPTER 5

Cane Corso vs. Other Breeds: What Makes the Cane Corso Breed Unique?

I f you are thinking of getting a Cane Corso, you may be thinking of its qualities compared to other breeds. It may be helpful if you have a more in-depth look at the Cane Corso in comparison with other dogs so you can understand the pros and cons of this breed vs. some other popular breeds.

Cane Corsos have some similarities with other large-breed dogs and also have some unique advantages regarding behavior, temperament, and upkeep. Some of the breeds that can be compared to a Cane Corso, or you may think about getting as an alternative to a Cane Corso, will be discussed thoroughly here to help you understand these differences.

Cane Corso puppies usually have blue eyes, especially the blue Cane Corsos.

Alaskan Malamute vs. Cane Corso

The Alaskan Malamute is a large purebred which originated from the United States. It is easy to mistake this dog for a wolf because of its appearance and markings, but it is a pure dog. Pet owners often describe this breed as independent and aggressive. Nevertheless, they are affectionate, friendly, loyal, playful, quiet, and social.

The Alaskan Malamutes are commonly black, gray, white, and also red. The Alaskan Malamute is famous for having a lot of talents that enable them to participate in different kinds of activities. Those things include carting, search and rescue operations, sled racing, sledding, and weight pulling. As of 2016, it ranks 59th in popularity, according to the AKC.

A Comparison Between the Alaskan Malamute and the Cane Corso

Between the Cane Corso and the Alaskan Malamute, the Corso will be easier to maintain because of its short coat. The grooming needs of a Cane Corso are not as demanding as the other breeds. That is why they are great for those people who do not have time and a large budget for grooming. When it comes to shedding the Alaskan Malamute sheds more than the Cane Corso.

Shedding is normal for many dogs as it's a natural process to lose old and damaged hair and replaces it with new hair. Some might find this off-putting because hairs can stick to upholstery and car seats. Regarding trainability, the Cane Corso is at an advantage.

Cane Corsos are great for owners who want a dog that can be trained and obey quickly. On the other hand, owners must have more patience in training the Alaskan Malamute and might need to find obedience or training schools for such a breed. When it comes to adaptability, both dogs are equally adaptable.

Regarding physical activity, the Alaskan Malamute would require more exercise, making them great companions for true health enthusiasts. Both dogs are not meant for novice owners; they require handlers with experience. The Alaskan Malamute is a better pet for kids, as it is a great playmate for them. A nasty trait of the Alaskan Malamute to consider is it's a notorious digger.

Australian Bulldog vs. Cane Corso

The Australian Bulldog is a large purebred dog. It is alert, intelligent, loving, and loyal. The most common colors for

Australian Bulldogs are apricot, brindle, fawn, orange, and white. The Australian Bulldog is regarded as a guard dog. The Australian Bulldog is a breed that came from a combination of several breeds. They are partly English Bulldog, Bullmastiff, Boxer, and partly English Staffordshire Bull Terrier.

Some might confuse its appearance with the English Bulldog. To find out whether it is an Australian Bulldog, the dog should have longer legs, less squished muzzle, and fewer wrinkles. These dogs may look like your average Bulldog, but they were selectively bred so that they can adapt well to the environment in Australia. Meanwhile, the Bulldogs, as their name already suggests, were bred to fight bulls and other large animals. Therefore, they are noticeably less reserved than other breeds, and the Australian Bulldog is no exception.

A Comparison Between the Australian Bulldog and the Cane Corso

The Cane Corso will be easier to maintain, and regular grooming is needed to keep its fur soft and shiny. Both the Cane Corso and Australian Bulldog shed moderately. To reduce shedding as well as make their coats softer and cleaner, regular brushing is advised. Training the Cane Corso will be easier in contrast to the Australian Bulldog, which is average when it comes to training. Australian Bulldogs gradually absorb information and require more patience.

When it comes to adaptability, the Cane Corso is better at responding and altering itself to adapt to the environment. However, Australian Bulldogs are better for kids because of their temperament. This is a suitable breed for kids because it is known to be playful and affectionate. Cane Corsos tend to be aloof and serious at first. Currently, the Australian Bulldog is still not accepted for recognition by the AKC.

Bloodhound vs. Cane Corso

The Bloodhound is another breed of giant and purebred dogs that are known for being affectionate, independent, and playful. The most common colors for Bloodhounds are black and tan, and red. To keep it healthy, it will need to get exercise regularly. It is a famous dog because of its uncanny abilities. The Bloodhound has varied uses. It participates in activities such as hunting, man trailing, narcotics detection, scent detection, search and rescue, and tracking.

The Bloodhound is also famous for being a scent hound. It has the capability to discern a human scent at great ranges and distances, even after a few days later. Its keen sense of smell, plus its strong and relentless tracking instinct, makes it a good police companion. The police and law enforcement from different parts of the world use this breed for tracking escaped prisoners, finding missing people, as well as lost children and pets. The Bloodhound is, in, fact so good at what it does that the evidence it uncovers can be used as evidence in court. Bloodhounds can certainly save the day. The Bloodhound ranked 11th in a survey of dogs that save lives.

A Comparison Between the Bloodhound and the Cane Corso

Both the Bloodhound and Cane Corso will be easy to maintain. As for the grooming needs, owners can rest assured that they do not have to spend much money for regular grooming.

When it comes to shedding, both the Bloodhound and Cane Corso experience moderate shedding. The Cane Corso is superior to the Bloodhound when it comes to ease of training. They can absorb information more effortlessly. Bloodhounds tend to be difficult to train, and they need a lot of patience and persistence from trainers. Both the Bloodhound and Cane Corso can equally adapt to new environments.

Bloodhounds and Cane Corso will require regular exercise. They should live an active life to remain fit. Bringing them to the dog park is a great idea, and other activities will be great for them to maintain overall health. Both the Bloodhound and Cane Corso are ideal for those who have previously owned dogs. Bloodhounds are known to be playful around kids and are much suitable as a children's pet or companion dog.

Border Collie vs. Cane Corso

Border Collies are popularly known because of their level of alertness, energy, and intelligence. They are also loyal, protective, and responsive. This breed usually has coats of the color black, gray, blue, brindle, and red.

Border Collies have double coats with a soft, thick undercoat and a rougher outer coat. It is a versatile dog that loves to do different kinds of activities that involve the use of agility and skills for competitive obedience, herding. It may also be used for detecting narcotics, scent, and during search and rescue.

The breed is commended for its skills in herding that are still evident today. They are still seen actively working in livestock fields and on farms worldwide. Aside from this, they are also one of the most high-energy dogs in the canine community. In fact, the Border Collie ranked 10th in a survey of dogs that save lives.

A Comparison Between the Border Collie and the Cane Corso

When it comes to maintenance, the Cane Corso will be easier to maintain. Border Collies belong to the long-haired variety and require professional grooming. The Cane Corso's grooming needs are manageable.

Both the Border Collie and Cane Corso shed moderately. Brushing can reduce shedding and make the coats softer and cleaner. Regarding trainability, both dogs are equal and will be easy to train.

The Cane Corso, however, is more adaptable to new situations and environments. The Border Collie will require more exercise, so they need owners who are home more often and can provide them the necessary physical activities.

Border Collies have the uncanny ability to escape from fenced yards so an owner must keep a watchful eye over them. The Cane Corso is less likely to stray from the perimeter of its territory. Border Collies are shy around strangers, but they still should be socialized since this shyness can also develop into aggression.

Boxer vs. Cane Corso

The Boxer is a large purebred that originated in Germany. It is known for being always being cheerful, alert, courageous, energetic, and playful. Their coats are commonly fawn, brindle patterning, and white. This breed is often used during military and police operations. They are also one of those breeds that are good at guiding blind people.

Aside from these qualities, they also are good at being sensitive seizure-alert dogs. They can succeed in agility, conformation, and obedience as well. Though this breed is known for being playful and patient with its family, they tend to be suspicious of strangers and become fearless when threatened. Because of its attributes, the Boxer ranked third in a survey of dogs that save lives.

A Comparison Between the Boxer and the Cane Corso

Both the Boxer and Cane Corso are easy to keep well-groomed. Since they both belong to the short-haired variety, owners who do not have to bring them to grooming parlors for dogs regularly. Boxers and Cane Corsos only shed moderately. Regarding trainability, the Cane Corso is superior and will learn new tricks and new commands quickly. The Boxer only has average trainability, compared to the Cane Corso. Both the Boxer and Cane Corso are quite adaptable to new situations and environments.

Both breeds require owners who will give them enough physical activity. The Boxer is better for kids because it would want to join in their play. Like Cane Corsos, Boxers make reliable watch dogs. Both the Cane Corso and the Boxer have a muscular and menacing appearance that will deter intruders. Boxers are more affectionate, however, and they never seem to outgrow their puppy stage and continue to seek out hugs and cuddles.

Dalmatian vs. Cane Corso

Both the Cane Corso and the Boxer have a muscular and menacing appearance that will deter intruders.

The Dalmatian is a large purebred best known for its spotted coat. Its salient traits include being aggressive, alert, energetic, friendly, independent, intelligent, loyal, outgoing, and playful. Dalmatians are black, brown, and white. Dalmatians require physical activity to be healthy.

Dalmatians are multi-talented dogs that like a wide array of activities such as endurance running, guarding, search and rescue, and tracking. Aside from traditional dog chores, Dalmatians are exceptional at circus performances and stage acts. This is due to their amazing memory. Dalmatian dogs are highly intelligent and willing to please, and as a result, they can be trained to do nearly any task.

A Comparison Between the Dalmatian and the Cane Corso

Both the Dalmatian and Cane Corso are easy to maintain because of their short coats. They will require minimal grooming. The Dalmatian sheds more and requires routine brushing. Regarding trainability, the Cane Corso is easier to train. The Cane Corso thrives on physical as well as mental challenges.

The Dalmatian only has average trainability compared to the Cane Corso. Dalmatians, however, are more adaptable and can integrate better in new situations and environments. Both dogs are active dogs and require physical activity to maintain their fitness.

The Dalmatian is better for novice dog owners, because they are less pushy compared to the Cane Corso. Dalmatians do well with kids because they have a naturally playful streak. If you have cats at home, the Dalmatian will be able to coexist with it more harmoniously than the Corso. Dalmatians, however, have a higher impulse to wander, so keeping them in a yard or a kennel when they are left alone is a good idea.

Doberman Pinscher vs. Cane Corso

The Doberman Pinscher was only first developed at the end of the 19th century. It is a new breed of dog, but has gained popularity through the years. The look of the Doberman is sleek and elegant. It's a very athletic dog. It is known for being intelligent, alert, and loyal. The Doberman is a courageous guard dog as well as a beloved family companion.

Dobermans tend to have a reputation as a very fierce dog, and this is further compounded by their look. This dog is stereotyped as being highly aggressive and vicious. The Doberman is bred to be a formidable guard dog, but it can also be gentle, watchful, and loving.

This dog does not go looking for trouble, but he is fearless and will defend his family and turf if he perceives danger. The Doberman Pinscher ranked fourth in a survey of dogs that save lives.

A Comparison Between the Doberman Pinscher and the Cane Corso

Regarding maintenance, both breeds are short-haired and therefore, easy to groom. They also shed only moderately. These dogs are equal in trainability; they will respond quickly to new commands and absorb information quickly. Overall, the Doberman Pinscher can better respond and alter itself to its environment. Thus, it has better adaptability. Both dogs require physical activity, and they should be guided by an owner to get their exercise requirements.

It is a good idea to socialize both dogs at an early age, so they will not grow to become aggressive. Have the puppies grow up with kids and provide them with a pleasant and relaxed experience; this is to ensure that they will grow up to be properly adapted to kids.

English Mastiff vs. Cane Corso

The Mastiff is commonly referred to as the "Mastiff" but can be more accurately called the English Mastiff or the Old English Mastiff. This dog is a giant purebred known for being affectionate, intelligent, protective, loyal to their owners, and social. It is a heavyweight and can weigh up to 175 to 200 pounds (79 kg to 91 kg). The most common colors for English Mastiffs are black and tan, brown, and silver. They need a lot of regular exercise, to stay healthy.

The Mastiff commonly participates in guarding and weight pulling. It has the "Mastiff" look, which is fearsome and can intimidate strangers and intruders. It certainly reflects its look since it was bred as a watchdog and guard dog. It will protect its territory. The Mastiff, however, is docile and gentle to those it considers as non-threatening.

A Comparison Between the English Mastiff and the Cane Corso

Both dogs belong to the Mastiff variety and are short-coated. Grooming should be easy and not demanding. The Mastiff and Cane Corso shed moderately. Again, the Cane Corso is superior in trainability, compared to the English Mastiff. The English Mastiff can be difficult to train and require more patience from the owners. Mastiffs have better adaptability, though, and can respond to alter themselves to their environment.

The Cane Corso requires more exercise, while the English Mastiff is more laid back and docile, and would require less physical activity. Both dogs require owners with previous dog ownership experience. Although gentle by nature, the English Mastiff should not be left alone with children due to its large size, which may cause untoward accidents. Another point to consider is that English Mastiffs can't be adapted well to apartment living because of their large size. They need space and confinement in a large yard.

German Shepherd vs. Cane Corso

German Shepherd Dogs were originally bred in Germany. They were used for herding large flocks of sheep by keeping order, as they swiftly and stealthily move with a strong demeanor. This breed is famed for having sound judgment and a stable temperament, which many breeds do not possess.

Because of these qualities, they become K-9 dogs that police bring during search and rescue and other operations. German Shepherds are naturally very protective. Owners train them early so that they will distinguish between families, friends, and strangers.

German Shepherds require a variety of activities and a huge space where they can run. Further, this breed grows to be devoted and loving to their family with proper training. They ranked 2nd in a survey of dogs that save lives. They have the special distinction of being the U.S. Army's official dog.

A Comparison Between the German Shepherd and the Cane Corso

The German Shepherd and Cane Corso do not require special grooming needs. German Shepherd sheds more, and they leave a trail of hair wherever they go. Both dog breeds are highly intelligent and have equal trainability. They are great for owners who want to obey commands and require well-behaved dogs.

The German Shepherd will require more physical activity compared to the Cane Corso, so they are better suited for owners who are home regularly and enjoy exercise. Both dogs are not for first-time owners, they require handlers with previous dog ownership experience.

Labrador Retriever vs. Cane Corso

Labrador Retrievers are among the most popular dog breeds out there today. They have a very good reputation. In fact, they ranked first in a survey of dogs that save lives! You probably see Labradors all around in most neighborhood yards. Looking into its traits like being friendly and not territorial, Labrador Retrievers are indeed ideal family pets. They will even get along with your cat.

They may be large in size, but Labrador Retrievers are seldom seen as hostile or aggressive with people. Rather, this breed can bond easily with most children and adults alike. Since they are "Retrievers," these breeds are the best in catching a Frisbee or a ball. They respond well while playing. Aside from this, they are also excellent at swimming and love to spend their time outdoors during the summer. They make wonderful companions for every activity.

A Comparison Between the Labrador Retriever and the Cane Corso

The Cane Corso will be easier to maintain compared to the Labrador. Cane Corso's grooming needs are less demanding. The Golden Retriever and Cane Corso shed moderately, and both dogs have a dense, water-repellent coat. Regarding trainability, both dogs are equal and highly intelligent. They will both respond to commands easily.

The Golden Retriever can adapt better and faster than Cane Corso. It has a more docile nature and can adapt to new situations, and other pets. Both the Golden Retriever and Cane Corso will require regular exercise. These dogs will need to remain active so that they will grow fit and healthy. They were both bred to do some work or activity. The Golden Retriever is better suited for novice owners because it has a more docile nature. Retrievers are better for kids because they are playful and gentle.

Pit Bull vs. Cane Corso

The American Pit Bull Terriers are purebreds that have descended from English Terriers and Bulldogs. They are known for qualities such as being affectionate, friendly, intelligent, and loyal. They have short, stiff coats and were bred for their speed and strength. Most of the time, the colors of American Pit Bull Terriers are black, black and tan, brown, and white. They may also be blue, red, and yellow. American Pit Bull Terriers need regular exercise.

Originally, they were used for baiting bears and bulls. They are versatile and can be used in activities such as agility, carting, competitive obedience, hunting, tracking, and weight pulling. This breed often gets a bad reputation for being an aggressive breed because it is often exhibited in illegal dog fighting. This is not true, though, because they can be of the most gentle-hearted breeds. Any dog will develop an aggressive streak, when mistreated. The Pit Bull may need extra socialization to ensure this, however.

A Comparison Between the Pit Bull and the Cane Corso

The American Pit Bull Terrier and Cane Corso will both be easy to maintain since they are short-coated. Like others, they do not need frequent grooming, for they shed moderately. Regarding trainability, both breeds are equal. They are ideal for those who want dogs to grasp information quickly and obey commands.

The American Pit Bull Terrier and Cane Corso are equally adaptable.

American Pit Bull Terriers require more exercise, so they need dedicated owners who can provide them the necessary activities. Both the American Pit Bull Terrier and Cane Corso are better suited for owners with previous dog ownership experience. American Pit Bull Terriers have a higher inclination to wander, so it's good to enclose them in a kennel or fenced yard. The American Pit Bull Terrier is not aggressive, but needs proper socialization and training early on.

Rottweilers vs. the Cane Corso

Rottweilers often get a bad reputation. They are stereotyped as feral looking dogs known for barking at the mailman. However, this breed has other qualities beyond being a very efficient guard dog that can deter intruders. They are also very trustworthy and make loyal pets.

Rottweilers are even-tempered and dignified companions. They do not trust newcomers easily. Rottweilers need time to decide who is worthy of their time and affection. With their families, they can be affectionate and playful.

Contrary to popular belief, Rottweilers are not a new breed. Though it has German heritage, its origins date back to the ancient Roman Empire. These dogs accompanied Roman armies as working dogs. Rottweilers have a short coat, and the only acceptable color is their distinct black and tan marking.

A Comparison Between the Rottweiler and the Cane Corso

Both the Rottweiler and Cane Corso will be easy to maintain due to their short coats. The Rottweiler and Cane Corso shed moderately. They will need regular brushing to reduce their shedding. Both dogs have equal trainability. Cane Corsos and Rottweilers are highly intelligent and can benefit from obedience training. The Cane Corso has better adaptability and can integrate itself to new situations in the environment.

Both dogs require physical activity, and they make great companions for equally active owners. Rottweilers and Cane

Corsos are better suited for owners with previous dog ownership experience. In adapting both breeds to children, it is best to socialize them and train them early on. Exposing them to kids as puppies will increase their acquiescence. Rottweilers tend to be more dominant and pushy, so it's good to establish boundaries with them early on and consistently to ensure a well-mannered dog.

Siberian Husky vs. Cane Corso

The Siberian Husky is a purebred dog, which is often found in Siberia, a region that has very cold temperatures. Because this breed is powerful, the Chukchi tribe that is also in Siberia used them for pulling sleds. They are also great for herding animals. The Siberian Husky is not possessive like other dogs, nor are they aggressive. It is their exotic and wolf-like appearance that makes them appealing to people.

This breed is known for having a variety of colors of various shades of gray and silver, black-and-white, sand, and red. Aside from this, the coats may also have striking markings on the head, which is unique to this breed. They have arresting eyes that seem to pierce right through anyone's heart. Aside from this, their even temperament, love of other dogs, as well as indifference to strangers are what make them welcome to the family environment.

A Comparison Between the Siberian Husky and the Cane Corso

The Cane Corso will be far easier to maintain. Siberian Huskies require regular grooming to make its fur always look good. Both the Siberian Husky and Cane Corso shed moderately. Regular brushing helps maintain the coat. The Cane Corso has superior trainability compared to the Siberian Husky. The Siberian Husky will require more exercise. They need owners who can provide them with the necessary physical activity. The Cane Corso, although it requires physical activity as well, knows when to be calm and peaceful.

Both dogs require experienced owners. Both the Siberian Husky and Cane Corso should be adapted to being raised with kids early on. Have the puppies grow up with children so they can be better adjusted to their presence. Siberian Huskies are more likely to wander and escape, so it's good to keep them in a fenced yard or kennel.

St. Bernard vs. Cane Corso

The Saint Bernard is a giant purebred known for being friendly, gentle, independent, intelligent, outgoing, quiet, and social. Indeed, its gentle look is telling of its inner qualities. It is the heaviest and largest breed of dog. In its full size, it can weigh up to 295 pounds (134 kg). Despite its appearance, the St. Bernard is a serene, unexcitable animal with an exalted reputation.

It ranked 12th in dogs that save lives. Legends surround this breed to this day of its rescue missions in the Swiss Alps. St. Bernards have either short or long coats that are often red, red with white, or brindle with white. To keep healthy, it will need to get exercise regularly. St. Bernards are used with people and other animals because they are raised to socialize. This way, they will not be aloof with strangers and other dogs.

A Comparison Between the Saint Bernard and the Cane Corso

The Cane Corso being short-haired will be easier to maintain. St. Bernards require moderate maintenance to keep their fur in good shape. Both the Saint Bernard and Cane Corso shed moderately.

Training the Cane Corso will be easier, and will be ideal for pet owners who like obedient dogs. On the other hand, Saint Bernards are willful and stubborn. Thus, they can be difficult to train, especially for first-time dog owners. Sometimes, this breed attentively listens, sometimes they don't.

The Cane Corso will require more exercise, Saint Bernards are more laid back and are a better choice for busy owners. Both dogs need to be socialized early on with kids so that they can grow used to them. Since they grow really big, Saint Bernards need proper training. The training should include socialization so that the dog will understand reasonable boundaries. Some Saint Bernards are not aware that they are big, that's why giving them a large room in areas they frequently go is a must.

Weimaraner vs. Cane Corso

The Weimaraner is a large purebred that are often alert, intelligent, loyal, and responsive. It comes in an elegant color of gray and silver. The Weimaraner was developed in Germany sometime in the early 1800s. It was developed as a hunting and companion dog, and there is some evidence that it originated from crossbreeding influences, including the Bloodhound.

Weimaraners need regular exercise. Weimaraners also have great talents in hunting. It is the best at pointing and tracking gundogs and retrievers. Aside from this, they are also sensitive and loving family companions.

The Weimaraner is often regarded as a reserved and elegant dog. It has a well-balanced body that is said to be good at gaining its bearing quickly. It is quick in learning, too. It is great for the family, because it has a personality and temperament that is energetic and affectionate. Weimaraner's are highly intelligent, and their potential can be unlocked further with proper training. They ranked 7th in a survey of dogs that save lives.

A Comparison Between the Weimaraner and the Cane Corso

Both the Weimaraner and Cane Corso will be easy to maintain. They have low maintenance grooming needs. Both the Weimaraner and Cane Corso shed moderately. Regarding trainability, both the Weimaraner and Cane Corso will be easy to train and are equally highly intelligent. This breed is good at listening and obeying the commands of its owner. That's why when training this breed; there is no need for continuous repetition.

Weimaraners will require more exercise. Therefore, it is a suitable companion to pet owners who love staying fit as well. Both breeds are better suited for owners with previous dog ownership experience. Weimaraners are better suited for families with children, because of their puppy-like attitudes.

Cane Corso Mix

Cane Corso Pit Bull Mix

One of the most prevalent mixes for the Cane Corso is the Cane Corso Pit Bull Mix. This mix results in an extraordinarily powerful dog. Though there are downsides in mixing the two, there are also positive aspects. One of the negative impacts of cross-breeding these two is the possibility of taking away some of their unique identities. For instance, their offspring may no longer have the ability to guard a house or property.

A Cane Corso Pit Bull Mix may be active in hunting prey. Thus, they require an owner with a high sense of authority. They should also understand their place in their human family.

Offspring of the two breeds often have differences from both breeds. Their weight ranges from 70 to 115 lbs (31.8 kg to 52.1 kg). These mixed breeds may not have special abilities, but they made great family pets if trained and socialized properly.

Cane Corso Mastiff Mix

The Cane Corso is also often mixed with the English Mastiff, which is a larger breed. Cane Corsos by themselves are very strong-willed, one-person dogs. They can be very territorial and require extensive socialization and obedience training, so that one can control them. Crossing the Cane Corso with the English Mastiff gives them more size, but it often it does very little to soften the temperament and "guard dog" abilities of the Cane Corso.

Not all these dogs are as edgy as the Cane Corso, some acquire more of the English Mastiff personality, and just like the American Mastiff, they can become wonderful dogs if properly handled and trained properly. This is, however, an unpredictable mixture.

CHAPTER 6

Cane Corso Puppies to Adults: How Can I Ensure a Smooth Transition?

The history of the Cane Corso describes a lively, energetic dog that is not afraid of any challenge. For dog owners, this temperament can work both ways. On the one hand, a consistent, self-assured owner giving proper care and disciplining the Corso from wandering, can train it to become a first-rate family dog. Wrong-handling, however, can turn it into an inappropriately aggressive dog that can pose a threat to the public.

With proper guidance, your Cane Corso can become gentle and friendly to people around it, including children. Start early, and you shouldn't have any problems!

Cane Corso Personality

With proper guidance, your Cane Corso can become gentle and friendly to people around it, including children. Developing a Corso into this ideal state requires regular training and socialization, starting at an early age. In other words, the Corso is not for households with members who dislike or are afraid of dogs. This dog is also not for anyone who cannot manage a big dog.

The domineering and highly intelligent traits of the Corso makes it easy for the dog to run out of control. This can be true, especially in a home where the owner does not exercise firm control and establish clear boundaries. The Corso will test the limits of what it's allowed to do. Hence, it is very important to set the rules with the dog from the very beginning, and make sure that all household members are advised as well. Your Corso must be made to understand that "nothing in life is free" by you demanding the performance of tasks like "sit" or "down," before giving it meals, treats, or a toy.

Attempting to instill discipline should not equate to hitting the dog, however. Doing so not only sends the wrong signal, but can also prove dangerous for such a big, powerful dog. Your Cane Corso is sensitive enough to understand its owner's tone of voice and can respond well to rewards and praise, as well as to firm, quick corrections, and consistent enforcement of the rules. A self-assured and calm disposition is the best attitude with the Corso. Consistency will allow it to relax and know who's in charge.

Is The Cane Corso Affectionate?

The Cane Corso has been known to be affectionate to its owners and come to the rescue when they feel their owners are being harassed. Many Cane Corsos attest to the affectionate nature of the dog. They describe the dog as friendly and affectionate with the family but aloof with strangers. The Cane Corso can certainly fulfill the role of cuddle buddy. It is a very loving and gentle giant that can easily slip into guard mode when something is fishy.

What are King Corso Puppies?

Cane Corso is also known as King Corso. The moniker King Corso refers to the Cane Corso, and it is the same breed.

Cane Corso Puppies or Italian Mastiff Puppies

The Cane Corso is also known as the Italian Mastiff, and Cane Corso puppies are the same as Italian Mastiff puppies. The Neopolitan Mastiff, which is an entirely different breed, is also sometimes incorrectly referred to as "Italian Mastiffs" as well. Cane Corsos and Neopolitan Mastiffs have distinctly different appearances.

While Cane Corsos start out as small puppies, they can grow fast with their big head size as puppies. They should be given toys and chew sticks as they love to chew and gnaw everything they can get their paws on. Cane Corso puppies are full of energy and thrive on human companionship.

Cane Corso Puppy's Temperament: What Qualities Should I Expect?

Training young Cane Corso puppies is relatively trouble-free as they are such intelligent, calm-natured, eager to please, and relatively attentive dogs. After learning something new, your Cane Corso tends to hold on to this new skill well. They can grow to become a big, powerful dog that is self-assertive and determined to accomplish whatever it starts. If properly trained to respect the owner and his rules, then the Corso's physical and mental prowess will work out for the best.

Full Grown Cane Corso Temperament

Adult Cane Corso dogs are intelligent and listen well to their owners. It is, therefore, important to train them properly. Correct and consistent training is the key to bringing out the best temperament in the Cane Corso.

Like all other dogs, the Cane Corso should be trained straight away, from an early age. This is a rule of thumb, and the Cane Corso is no exception. Only by properly training and socializing a puppy Cane Corso in its youth can it become a well-trained adult when the day comes.

Ideally, the Cane Corso can become very devoted to its owner and wishes only to please its owner when it has been subjected to such a training regimen. Also of utmost importance is teaching a Cane Corso to acknowledge you the owner as the alpha. Otherwise, the dog might want to assert dominance and become aggressive.

Being strong and firm without resorting to physical violence to punish them is the best way to handle the Cane Corso. Punishing them with force will make them respect the owner less and lead them to exhibit more aggression to strangers.

Positive reinforcement works better in making the Cane Corso more responsive. When the dog does something positive, it should be given a treat, congratulated with a pat, and spoken to in a positive tone.

CHAPTER 7

How Do I Prepare My Home for a Cane Corso?

F rom a Cane Corso puppy's first day, the house must already be designed to fit its needs. Upon its arrival, the Cane Corso puppy must be habituated to regular meals. Particular feeding techniques and a sense of regularity must be enforced on the puppy. This means scheduling the feeding so as to allow the puppy to be fed regularly until it gradually becomes accustomed to living according to a timetable.

For Your Cane Corso puppy's first day in your home, you should ensure that you prepare the environment properly ahead of time.

Cane Corso Puppy's Dish

A Cane Corso puppy should be fed in the following way: Place a bowl of food on a vertical stand equipped with a stable fixture that is equal or a little higher than a puppy's chest. This should make it convenient for the puppy to lower its muzzle inside the bowl so that its back will stand erect, and it will not have to have to bend too low.

The feeding bowl that will be used for the puppy must be aluminum, ceramic, or enameled. This should not have any defects, dents, or granulations so as to avoid cuts.

To ensure that your Cane Corso's paws will not slide over the floor, a small rug should be placed under them. Alongside the feeding bowl, a separate bowl should be allocated for its water.

The bowl of water can either be placed opposite the food stand or on the same single stand. The height of the water bowl can be regulated like the food stand. The dog's drinking water should be changed 2-3 times a day to keep it fresh and clean.

Cane Corso Dog Collar

Dog collars for use by your Cane Corso should be divided according to their particular use.

First are the soft collars that are used for walking. This classic collar is made of leather, synthetic materials, or a combination thereof. To give the dog additional comfort, these collars may have special interior padding made of thick felt, fleece, or thin leather and may come with a soft filler.

Second is the protection training collar equipped with a special handle for better control that allows the owner to hold the dog back.

Third are guarding collars, used for dogs that are always leashed. This needs to be quite reliable, and should thus be more durable than the rest.

Fourth are choke collars, whether leather, metal chain, or synthetic, that are used mainly for training or as show collars. They are light weight, however, also makes them comfortable and great for everyday use. The collar's choking effect can be perceived by the dog in the same manner a mother in a pack teaches its cubs by slightly choking their necks. However, this should be applied to dogs sparingly and correctly, lest they lose their pedagogic value. Consulting an experienced instructor is advisable before using such a collar and the types of actions that can be applied to a dog.

And fifth are pinch collars that feature spikes. These can create discomfort for the dog if the tension is too strong, and should thus be used only under the strict supervision of experienced instructors.

Remember that putting collars on the Cane Corso constantly is not recommended, as this can create discomfort by rubbing the dog's fur. If it is necessary to hold the dog at home, then using a thin leather knot is advisable.

A dog training collar is ideally placed behind the ears and under the jaws. Given the Cane Corso's dominant traits and large size, it is necessary to acquire effective, high-quality collars. Nevertheless, there should be no illusion that using collars in real life is easy. Flat collars can loosen, chain collars may slide down the neck, and choke collars can hold the dog back without them learning anything. Caution must always be exercised when it comes to training the Cane Corso.

Cane Corso Harness

A good alternative to the collar is a harness, which makes less discomfort because it is wrapped around the dog's body. The dog-friendly design of a harness prevents causing stress or injury to the dog, while keeping it comfortable. Many trainers prefer harnesses to collars, as they lessen the possibility of a neck and/or tracheal injury.

A harness is a multifunctional tool that can be used for training, walking, and working with a Cane Corso of any age and size. A light-reflective dog harness is also an excellent choice for pleasant walks that will make it easier for owners to watch over the dog in the dark. This is the perfect dog-training device for keeping them visible and safe at night.

Cane Corso Toys

Rubber Dog Ball for Cane Corso Training

Ultimately, even an adult Cane Corso is a little puppy inside. It adores toys and would thus greatly appreciate a rubber dog ball for both playing and training.

Durable Dog Fire Plug for Cane Corsos

A dog fire plug can be used to help stop the Cane Corso from always begging for treats. This not only helps in slowing down the dog's feeding process but also livens up its everyday routine. Treats or kibbles can be placed in a hole inside the dog fire plug. The dog should be allowed to chew the toy until it gets the treat.

CHAPTER 8

Cane Corso Food and Nutrition: What's Important?

Because the Cane Corso is a relatively large dog, it needs quite a large quantity of high-quality food. Quality nutrition is needed to keep it vigorous and in optimum health, and protein is especially important.

Because the Cane Corso is a relatively large dog, it needs considerable amounts of food.

Nutritional Needs

An active adult Cane Corso that weighs 90 pounds, for example, would need an average of 2,100 calories as daily caloric intake. But spayed, neutered, or older dogs may require fewer calories.

However, more calories are needed for some dogs depending on their metabolism and level of activity. A growing puppy, for instance, can consume more calories than adult dogs. Another example is a young adult Cane Corso with a weight of 90 pounds, requiring an estimated 2,164 calories every day.

Because protein is crucial to a Cane Corso's diet, it is advised to give growing puppies a minimum of 22 percent protein while adult dogs should get at least 18 percent protein for maintenance. Fortunately, most dog foods that are good quality will surpass these percentages. One of the Cane Corso's important source of energy is fat. This should comprise at least 8 percent of a Cane Corso puppy and 5 percent of the adult dog's diet.

Protein

It is ideal to select dog food that features at least two or three meat proteins. Meat meals and whole types of meat like whole beef, chicken, fish, lamb, and pork are also good sources of protein. However, normal water moisture is contained in whole meats since animals are about 70 percent water. Meat meals are also acceptable first ingredients in any good quality dog food.

Carbohydrates

While it is not necessary to feed a dog food with excessively high protein content, it is highly recommended to keep the carbohydrate percentage from low to moderate.

Fats

The Cane Corso requires good sources of fat since some vitamins needed by the dog are only fat-soluble. But since fat varies in quality depending on its source, it is necessary to look for high-fat sources like chicken fat.

Fish oil can also provide omega-3 fatty acid that can help keep the dog's skin and coat healthy. Docosahexaenoic acid or DHA is a specific type of omega-3 fatty acid that helps with brain development for puppies. More mature dogs can benefit from medium chain triglycerides where medium-chain fatty acids (MCFAs) can be found. Made from a combination of coconut and other oils, MCFAs can help older dogs act and feel younger.

Dry Food

Your Cane Corso dog can be fed a certain amount of food depending on its age, sex, size, and activity level. In general, an adult Cane Corso can consume 5 to 10 pounds of quality kibble a week. This means serving 4 to 8 cups of kibble allocated into two feedings every day.

Canned Food

Adding fresh food or a good probiotic supplement can help boost the nutritional value of canned food or commercial kibble for the dog. Probiotics can help keep the Cane Corso's intestines healthy and efficient, and this is also where a large part of the dog's immune system activity occurs. Dogs that mainly feed on commercial dog chow would also benefit from mineral supplements and whole food vitamins since food bought from the dog store does not normally contain sufficient vitamins and minerals.

Homemade Food

It is advisable to feed your Cane Corso a home-cooked meal at least once or twice a week. Some easy steps to do this are as follows:

Begin by boiling a whole chicken until it is tender, then pull all the meat from the chicken bones. Drop some scrambled raw eggs into the boiling broth next. Finally, finish up with a kettle-full of rice. While cooking, add a little oil. The end-product is rice in chicken broth, with shreds of chicken and pieces of egg mixed in. The ingredients can also be mixed up for variety. This can be done with sliced potatoes, pasta, and other assorted fresh vegetables. Other recipes can also be experimented with.

Raw Bones are Healthy

Raw bones, which are softer, digestible, natural, and nutritional, are healthy for the Cane Corso. A cooked bone, on the other hand, will become brittle and hard, losing most of its nutritional value. Cooked chicken bones should never be fed to a Cane Corso. They will break into fatally sharp splinters and fragments that can kill the dog. However, raw chicken bones are good.

The raw game, pork meat, or bones should be frozen completely for three weeks before feeding them to the dog. This measure will kill parasite larva that may be present in the meat.

Treats

Young, energetic Cane Corso puppies would enjoy fun toys and chew toys. These should always be made available not only to provide pleasure and entertainment, but also to help them with the teething process.

Avoid rawhide strips. Though they are commonly available treats, but rawhide strips are often laced with harsh chemicals that can be unhealthy for the Cane Corso. Natural chemical-free rawhide strips should also be ingested in moderation and limited amounts. A large quantity of the substance will swell in the dog's stomachs and can result in bloating or blockages.

Raw bones, on the other hand, are good for teething and should have no side effects.

Food to Avoid

In general, it is best to avoid food with sweeteners, artificial colors, and preservatives. Doing this helps keep the dog's immune system stronger. Take care to feed your dog well to keep them healthy. You may save a couple of dollars on cheap kibble brands, but it will be at the expense of your dog's life and health. Home-cooked and raw diets are also better than processed dog foods, the quality of which cannot be guaranteed.

CHAPTER 9

What are Some of the Common Health Problems of a Cane Corso and How Can I Avoid Them?

Canine Hip Dysplasia is the abnormal or defective development of a dog's hip. This abnormal growth of the hip results in excessive wear of the dog's joint cartilage during weight bearing. This will eventually lead to arthritis, a degenerative joint disease, or osteoarthritis. This is a developmental disease that is not present at birth, but is acquired as the dog ages.

Like other dogs of the mastiff breed, the Cane Corso commonly encounter eye and other health problems.

Hip Dysplasia

Canine Hip Dysplasia

This defect is considered to have a genetic base, which gives the Cane Corso a predisposition as to the manner its hips are formed during birth as well as how much laxity there is in the joint. But, studies demonstrate that the dog's environment also plays a significant role in the possibility of dysplasia setting in.

In other words, dogs predisposed to hip dysplasia do not necessarily develop symptoms if not for particular environmental conditions. Avoiding obesity and providing proper nutrition is the best deterrent to this dysplasia. Meanwhile, too much exercise can also lead to damaged joints. Hip dysplasia is relatively common to the Cane Corso breed and should always be considered owners in training and rearing the dog.

Epilepsy

Idiopathic Epilepsy

While seizure disorders are fairly common among canines, one of the most upsetting causes for dogs to suffer seizures is the condition called idiopathic epilepsy. Unlike seizures caused by brain tumors or exposure or ingestion of toxic materials, the cause of this disorder, from the word idiopathic itself, is unknown. This can be diagnosed after a veterinarian conducts blood and urine tests to determine the presence of toxins and rules out other causes.

A Cane Corso usually begins to exhibit symptoms of idiopathic epilepsy at the age of 2 years old, although this may already set in as young as nine months or as late as five years old. Caution is advised in approaching a Cane Corso during or immediately after a seizure. Dogs may experience blindness and extreme disorientation after seizures and may become afraid or aggressive. A seizure may last from a few seconds up to 20 minutes or even more. It is advisable to give the dog space for itself and make sure it has regained control of itself before venturing to comfort it.

Mange

Demodex Mange

Demodicosis is caused by a variety of Demodex mite species and can be seen in both cats and dogs. The skin of all animals, including humans, have Demodex mites and typically reside in small numbers inside the hair follicles. With all animals possessing these mites, the Demodex mange is not deemed to be contagious. Animals acquire these mites from their mothers in the process of nursing.

That said, those animals that do get Demodex mange may have an acquired or inherited immune system defect that fails to keep in check the number of Demodex mites. This results in an explosion of the mite population, crowding not only the hair follicles but also resulting in adverse bacterial infections. The mites produce other substances that further damage the immune system, thus perpetuating the infestation.

Demodex mite infestation is thus an effect and not the cause of this health condition. Rather than focusing simply on eliminating the mites, more attention should be given to addressing the cause of the immune system deficiencies. This condition is mostly the result of an inherited incompetence in the immune system in young animals. But emotionally challenging situations, as well as hormone fluctuations, can also cause a Demodex mange outbreak. Many times, the dog's health will return to normal once such temporary stresses to their immune system, like first heat cycles in female dogs, are removed.

Eyelid Abnormalities

Like other dogs of the mastiff breed, the Cane Corso commonly encounter eye problems. Some of the most common eye defects encountered by the Cane Corso and its molosser relatives are ectropion, entropion, and the glandular hypertrophy or "cherry eye."

Ectropion is the rolling out of the lower eyelid that exposes the sensitive tissues found beneath it. The exposed tissue of the 3rd eyelid is prone to become inflamed and infected, resulting in what is called the "exposure conjunctivitis." This often caused by the correction of entropion or sometimes in conjunction with entropion wherein the eyelid rolls inward. While unpleasant to the human eye, ectropion is not particularly dangerous to the animal's health except when infection occurs.

Entropion, mentioned earlier, is the opposite of Ectropion. Entropion is the inward curling of the eyelid, which leads to the lashes scratching the cornea and causing irritation. If left unchecked, this can result in the eventual scarring and ulceration of the eyes. This happens because the eyeball is too small for the eye socket, causing the lids to roll into the eye.

Entropion symptoms include irritated red eyes, tear stains on the dog's face, and constant eye-watering. This condition is hereditary and commonly affects the lower lid. However, the upper lid may also be affected, and one or both eyes may suffer the condition. It is necessary to conduct surgery to correct the entropion and save further scarring of the cornea.

Glandular hypertrophy takes place when the 3rd eyelid gland is swollen, inflamed, and protrudes from the lower lid. This is often called the "cherry eye" because of the condition's resemblance to the fruit. This can happen to one or both eyes. This is common among dogs below one-year-old. Removing the gland is the most successful way to treat the condition. The surgical reposition and tracking of the gland often does not end successfully and often results in the eventual removal of the gland.

Distichiasis if the abnormal growth of eyelashes, inside the eyelid themselves. This disorder often comes and goes and is unnoticeable by the average owner until the dog's eye undergoes excessive tearing. Symptoms also include excessive blinking, inflammation, and other discharges. If left unchecked, the dog may paw the sore eye or keep it tightly closed.

Bloat

Gastric Torsion

Bloating is a common life-threatening condition for large breed dogs. While diagnosis is often simple, pathological changes in the dog's body may make treatment expensive, complicated, and not always successful. Bloating is more prone among big, deep-chested dogs that commonly eat once a day while being in the habit of gobbling food, gulping air, drinking massive amounts of water right after eating, and exercising forcefully after feeding.

Pre-gloat or simple gastric distention is common among young puppies predisposed towards overeating. However, it can occur in any dog breed or age. Symptoms will include signs of obvious pain and frequent looking at the stomach, which will look swollen. Pre-gloat is often relieved by belching gas or vomiting food. Prevention is key by feeding your dog twice a day and discouraging it from rapid food intake. Vigorous exercise should also be disallowed just two hours after a meal.

Inborn Immunity vs. Vaccinations

Like other dogs, a Cane Corso has two types of immunity against infectious diseases. First is inborn immunity transmitted from the mother to her puppy. Second is evoked immunity because of vaccination or after the dog's body develops resistance to a disease it got infected with.

The effectiveness of inborn immunity subsides, thus making it necessary to have the Cane Corso puppy vaccinated against infectious diseases. An experienced veterinarian should be consulted with regards to vaccinations. The dog must be given an individual vaccination schedule.

The latent or still hidden stage of a lot of diseases can last for about two weeks. In this period, before the dog receives any vaccination, cautiousness should be observed, especially during walks. It would be best to avoid contact with other dogs, cats, or strangers who want to stroke the dog.

It is important to remember that the 2-week period before vaccination should serve as an extraordinary quarantine for the Cane Corso puppy. It should be carefully protected in this 14-day period from psychic tension, fright, and any untoward environmental conditions.

Vaccination against some of the most dangerous dog diseases like hepatitis, plague, leptospirosis, rabies, and viral enteritis must be done once a year.

After the vaccination, the Cane Corso can be walked outside again. However, quarantine time should be extended a little in cold climates, or in cases when your dog inevitably interacts with adult dogs in the yard.

The Cane Corso puppy should be examined by a veterinarian if it begins to exhibit symptoms like diarrhea, excessive salivation, nasal discharge, apathy, asthenia, and deafness after vaccination.

CHAPTER 10

How Do I Train My Cane Corso?

Being a highly trainable and intelligent dog, the Cane Corso can be made to do what you want in various ways. The key is providing leadership. To do this, it would be best to start by giving obedience classes. This should decrease the puppy's leaning to exhibit dominance and aggression. The most current theory on dog training today emphasizes positive training over the use of force.

Being a highly trainable and intelligent dog, the Cane Corso can be made to behave quite well with a little patience.

Neutering is also not the best answer to handling aggression. While it may help in some cases, this does not always work.

What are the Common Behavioral Problems of Your Cane Corso?

Teaching bite inhibition to the Cane Corso is of utmost importance. This is crucial — even if the puppy is already well-socialized and has learned bite inhibition with its mother and littermates. This issue has become controversial as some trainers recommend "scuffing" the dog when it bites while others oppose this measure.

If the Cane Corso puts its teeth on you while playing, remove your hand, tell it "no," and stop playing with the dog for at least 5 minutes. The dog will be upset at the loss of its playmate, thus eliminating the need to scuff it.

The Cane Corso should never be encouraged to become aggressive. The breed serves as a natural guard dog and is already commonly suspicious of strangers, other animals, and even objects sometimes. It should not be necessary to teach the dog to be wary of new situations. Encouraging or excessively praising the dog when it is acting aggressive and nervous, growling or barking, will only lead to bringing up a disproportionately aggressive dog.

How to Train the Cane Corso Puppy

The owner has the responsibility of teaching a Cane Corso its proper place in the household. This means starting on the first day by holding the puppy on his back in your arms, say when watching TV or just hanging out. This can help the puppy to get used to acquiesce to you in a non-confrontational manner.

If the puppy gets it into its head to become the alpha, it will begin to exhibit dominant behavior. It will increasingly growl or snap when it is picked up, moved, or when someone gets near its toys or food. It will growl or snap when it does not want to be placed outside or doesn't want to head in a particular direction. Another expression of dominance is when it mounts or humps family members. This must be immediately restrained by quick action.

Getting angry isn't the best move as this can break the puppy's spirit. Reacting to aggression with anger and fear may unnecessarily agitate the puppy and lead to a worsening of its negative behavior. Confidently and assertively set the tone, lead by example, and allow the puppy to take cues from you.

First correction: Loudly tell the puppy "no" while looking at it directly and moving into its space. Grab its collar to protect yourself from getting bitten. Try to give a clear impression of having had enough, then release it and go about your business. Never pet the puppy or reassure it that things are okay, as this will only reinforce negative behavior. Praise and reassurance should be reserved for positive behavior only.

Second Correction: The physical touch becomes necessary when the puppy continues growling or snapping without provocation. Assert yourself by forming your hand into a "claw," all the while establishing contact with its ear and neck. This action simulates the type of correction that dominant dogs use in a pack. However, be warned that this technique must be seen through to the end. Committing to this step means not stopping until achieving the desired effect of the puppy averting its eyes and subduing aggression. Maturity is an important consideration here. An eight-week-old puppy is not the same with an eighteen-week old puppy which by then should already know who the boss is.

Added Correction: it is normal to encounter a strong-willed puppy occasionally. Always consider that the things covered here are the foundation of dog discipline. If the puppy continues to test you, this will have to be matched consistently. If, for example, the puppy tests you and gets what it wants, it will only grow to be more confident. The important thing is to be consistent in order not to reinforce bad behavior by allowing it. Winning all battles means never losing the war. As always, confident, consistent, and quick correction is fundamental.

Over Bonding

It is also important to note that Cane Corso puppies need time alone by themselves during the day to help them develop self-confidence and a sense of safety even without its owner, from an early age. This should be made clear to members of the household, especially if someone is home with the puppy most of the time. A puppy will become fearful if it becomes too dependent on its owner. Strike a balance between the puppy given time to bond with the family and time to be fearless, alone.

Do not carry or hold the Cane Corso puppy all of the time. Owners must resist treating puppies like babies, even if they are so sweet and cute. If the puppies are carried extensively or allowed to sit or sleep on their master's lap for hours on end, they might develop two things. First, they will become too dependent on the owner. Second, they will become fearful when they are

Mark Manfield

alone without their master's presence. Puppies must be loved and kissed and cuddled. But they must also be put down and taught how to stand on their own.

How to Housebreak the Cane Corso

Two basic rules in housebreaking a dog are as follows. First, it's the owner's fault if the puppy potties in the house. This simply means the puppy was not watched well enough. Secondly, consistency should be maintained.

Cane Corso puppies require pottying after eating, after waking, and after playtime. To be successful, the owner must know when they need to go out to potty, while containing them properly in case they don't. If it is impossible to watch the puppy the whole time it is inside the house, place it outside or in a crate to play.

In the beginning, the Cane Corso puppy must be restricted to areas in the house in the master's line of sight. When it's potty time, the puppy should be picked up and accompanied by the owner outside. One of the biggest errors made by folks is not going with the puppy.

Bring your puppy to an area in the yard where it has become used to, and set it down. Command the puppy to potty in a positive tone. In time, it will understand the correlation between the command and the act as it grows older. Soon it can potty on command. Setting a schedule for sleeping and feeding will help in knowing when the dog needs to go for a potty. Never get angry. Don't rub noses or swat it with paper. If the puppy goes in the house, it is the owner's fault for failing to watch close enough, or for not sticking to the schedule.

What Is the Importance of Socialization For Your Cane Corso?

It is important for a Cane Corso to be socialized at an early age. They must begin socialization, even as puppies, as this is the dog's "imprinting" period. If the puppy is just kept locked in a kennel or is not taken out of its new home, the puppy may become nervous around anyone or anything unfamiliar.

Your Corso puppies should be taken out and walked around to meet other people, and other dogs, even before their last set of vaccines have been taken. The best opportunity for teaching the dog will be missed, when this socialization period is over.

While the Cane Corso can be socialized during its entire life, even this cannot make up for early socialization. Never being taken out of the yard in its first four months will make a puppy shy and things especially difficult for the owner.

The dog should be socialized as an adult to reduce shyness and lessen the possibility of its developing aggressive behavior, especially it it was not properly socialized during its early years. Shyness can be inherited or learned by the Cane Corso, which may run, hide, or bite. A bag of its favorite treats should be brought along during the daily walk with the dog.

CHAPTER 11

What is the Proper Grooming Routine for My Cane Corso?

The Cane Corso is a low-maintenance dog with regards to grooming. The dog is a light shedder, making the maintenance of its coat a simple affair. A quick wipe-down with a damp cloth followed by an occasional once-over with a soft-brush is often all the coat-care the dog will need.

The Cane Corso is a low-maintenance in the area of grooming.

The Corso's toenails should be trimmed, beginning at a very young age, to make the routine familiar to the dog before it reaches its owner's size. Regular dental care is also no different for the Corso from that of any other large-breed dog.

Cane Corso Grooming: The Basics

First, it should be noted that a Cane Corso has a light undercoat that becomes heavier during the cold winter months, and a short flat coat characterized by being stiff and shiny.

Second, the Cane Corso's coat is completely waterproof. The coat won't absorb water. Not having the ability to keep the water in its fur often helps in avoiding a mess. The dog can run around outside in the rain and won't come in the house wet and dripping.

Grooming should be done for 4 to 8-week intervals for the cleaning of ears, clipping of nails, checking of anal glands, and ensuring the coat and skin are in healthy condition.

The Cane Corso's eyes should be bright and alert. A special eye wash that can be bought from pet stores should be used during bath time to flush out any foreign objects.

Monthly cleaning is advised for the dog's ears to ensure that no ear problems requiring veterinary attention will arise. However, cleaning should be done only as far as can be seen with the eye, never further.

A balm should be applied weekly to the paws to keep the paw pads pliable and soft. This should make the pads less likely to crack and dry.

A shedding blade would also be needed to pull out the dead coat. Short coated breeds like the Corso shed all year round and must constantly be brushed.

CHAPTER 12

Cane Corso Dogs for Sale: What Should I Look For?

At this point, one of your first considerations should be whether you will get either a puppy or a full-grown dog. Puppies are no doubt adorable—their look and playful attitude can certainly melt your heart. But a puppy will also require lots of your time and attention, especially during the first year of its life. You will be responsible for everything, including meeting all of its needs and training it to behave properly. The way you care for your puppy will be a big factor in shaping its behaviors and traits.

Adopting an adult Cane Corso will allow you to bypass the puppy stages that can be difficult or even destructive, such as teething and potty training.

Should I Buy a Puppy or a Full-Grown Dog?

Meanwhile, getting an adult dog has its advantages. Adopting an adult Cane Corso will allow you to bypass the puppy stages that can be difficult or even destructive, such as teething and potty training. It may not be necessary to put the dog through basic obedience class or to housetrain them, although this depends on their history and prior training experience. You will just need to get the dog used to your family's new routine, and then it will be ready to be your canine companion.

In short, there are pros and cons to weigh for both options. Here are some points to consider before you decide.

The first thing you should ask is: How much time can you devote to raising and training your new companion? Raising a puppy entails constant oversight—you'll have to keep them out of danger and mischief, especially during their first few months. You'll also have to take the puppy to obedience training classes to lay the groundwork for their good behavior. Those who work at home or have sufficient free time are well-suited to getting a puppy. If you have a busy schedule, consider an adult dog that has already been housetrained and can be well-behaved in your absence.

Also, think about your lifestyle. Are you more of a homebody, or are you out and about for most of your typical day? If you spend most of your time at home, your lifestyle may be more conducive to raising a puppy. But if you usually have a packed social calendar, an adult dog who is already trained may be a better match.

Another question is: How important is it that you raise the dog yourself? Raising a puppy yourself means you greatly influence its personality and behavior. In contrast, an adult dog will already have a fairly established personality, and its history may have caused it to develop behavior patterns that you consider undesirable. If you prefer a greater ability to shape your dog's personality to fit into your household, a puppy is more suitable.

If your household includes babies or young toddlers, consider waiting a few years before getting a dog (whether puppy or adult). Young children can unintentionally harm animals; but when kids are somewhat older, they can help with the tasks involved in raising a puppy or taking care of an adult dog. If you get an adult, choose one that was raised around children and that will tolerate kids' playfulness.

Finally, does cost matter? There are expenses associated with both puppies and adults, but it often costs hundreds of dollars more to buy a purebred puppy than to get an adult or a rescue dog. If cost is a serious consideration, adopting may be a better option.

How to Find and Recognize Good Cane Corso Breeders

When you are ready to buy a Cane Corso, it is good to know a good breeder and the tell-tale signs of bad Cane Corso breeders. Your Cane Corso will be there with you for life. It is a strong-willed breed, and you should know the temperament and health concerns of the individual pup you are getting.

First of all, good breeders have a thorough knowledge of their breed. They have spent time and effort in understanding the breed's history, temperament, health considerations, and standard. They should be willing and able to answer your questions and provide you with information on the benefits and drawbacks of the dog you plan to get.

A good breeder should educate potential owners about their breed. Look for a breeder who specializes in one to two breeds only. They should be aware of any special requirements of the breed.

Good breeders know their dog's weaknesses. Breeders who can recognize a dog's faults are better equipped to plan for the ideal breeding that will result in improvements in the succeeding generation.

Good breeders plan their breeding. They should be able to explain how they chose the sire and dam of each breeding they produce, including the strengths and weaknesses of both sire and dam and their reasons for choosing those specific dogs to complement each other to maximize the chances that the next generation of pups will be superior to both the sire and dam.

Breeders should not have a constant supply of available puppies. Good breeders put thought and effort into considering each litter they produce, caring for them, and finding a good home for each pup. You may have to wait before you get your puppy, but if it is from a dependable breeder, it will be worth the wait.

A good breeder asks you questions and screens the future home of the puppy. They make sure each puppy is well placed in a suitable, loving, responsible home. Because they want to make sure they find the right home for each pup, good breeders have a careful screening process that includes asking about your lifestyle, your family, your other dog/s, and your experience with raising dogs.

Look for someone who breeds for health and who will stand behind their pups. Good breeders know the health issues that commonly affect their breed, and this knowledge is the basis for carefully building a breeding program on a foundation of healthy dogs. If a dog is known to carry or produce a serious genetic health issue, a good breeder will be willing to spay/neuter this dog and remove them from their program.

All breeders should register their puppies through a trustworthy registry, such as the American Kennel Club (AKC), the Fédération Cynologique Internationale (FCI), or their recognized affiliates.

Good breeders should also provide a Full Health Guarantee and a clear Contract. These documents signify that the breeder fully stands behind the puppies they produce and also protect the buyer as well as the seller.

Breeders should take full responsibility for every single pup they produce. Having played a huge role in bringing a dog into the world, they are responsible for ensuring that the dog has a safe and loving home and does not end up abused or abandoned. This is the most significant commitment that breeders take.

Finally, great breeders go beyond taking responsibility for their dogs. These are the breeders who actively participate in rescue efforts to help ensure that other dogs of their breed will find a good home.

The Signs of Bad Cane Corso Breeders

On the other end of the spectrum are bad Cane Corso breeders whom you should avoid. If the puppy has no parents or the breeder refuses to let you meet its parents, this is a sign of a bad breeder. In fact, this person may not even have bred the puppy themselves, but may be selling him secondhand without telling you.

Beware of breeders who insist on "meeting somewhere" if you request to visit the kennel. You should be able to see where your puppy was born.

Avoid breeders who offer five or more different breeds and their mixes. Remember that reputable breeders only focus on one breed, or two at most.

Ask questions about the puppy's and its parents' vaccination. Bad breeders probably do not have their puppies, and even adult dogs vaccinated. Another possibility is that the breeder has so many puppies that they get mixed up and get some puppies vaccinated twice.

Check the puppy and its surroundings for cleanliness. If a puppy smells like a kennel and has poor coat quality, it may be a sign that it came from a puppy mill.

Bad breeders don't care about what happens to each puppy in the long run, whether the buyer will care for it or end up dumping it in a shelter. This is why reputable breeders have documents including a health contract and a request that you return the dog to them if things do not work out.

A final telling sign is giving you the puppy before it is eight weeks old—the minimum age that you should take a pup from its mother and littermates. A breeder who sells puppies early may be avoiding the costs of feeding them and giving them shots.

Cane Corso Adoption or Cane Corso Rescue

Getting an adult Cane Corso through adoption or rescue is another good option. Most Cane Corso rescue groups rely on foster homes to ensure that dogs for adoption are trained to behave well indoors. Aside from already being trained, they have longer attention spans than puppies so that any additional teaching will be easier and faster.

If you have children in your family, you can select a dog who will get along with them because they already act friendly. Also, an adult dog's needs for attention and playtime are much less demanding than those of a puppy.

Adopting an adult dog is truly a good deed. Many people avoid adopting adult dogs—one common reason is that they assume that Cane Corsos in shelters have ended up there because they have severe behavior or health issues. However, the majority of Cane Corsos in shelters are there because their previous owner realized that they simply do not have the time, money, or patience to care properly for the animals. Others were lost and simply never found by their original owners. These dogs are generally in good health and eager to please their new owners.

How Much Does a Cane Corso Cost?

If you are getting a puppy from a good breeder, who researches and provides detailed information on pedigrees, health, and temperament, the price of a Cane Corso may range from $1,500 up to $4,000. Potential owners who are interested in a breed/show-quality should expect the cost to be at the higher end of that range. Have an in-depth discussion with your breeder regarding the quality of their pups and the price they are asking for it. Research and compare different breeders. Analyze conformation and temperament. Remember to canvass and look around.

Cane Corso Breeders

There are plenty of Cane Corso Breeders on the internet. You can find one in your local area by searching ads in the newspaper and visiting kennel clubs so you can network with people who can give you good advice about the best breeders around.

Best Cane Corso Breeders

Good Cane Corso breeders do research on the type of dog they produce. In this chapter, we have discussed the signs of good Cane Corso breeders, and previously we have discussed the standards and conformation of the greed. Establish the price you are willing to pay for a Cane Corso and ask around for a good Cane Corso breeder who will charge you fairly for a pup. Don't hurry, and take your time to find a quality dog.

Cane Corso Mastiff for Sale

It is good to look into your local area or over the internet for a reputable breeder. Cane Corsos are also known as Italian Mastiffs, so they may be listed that way. Cane Corso pups can be taken home at eight weeks of age.

CHAPTER 13

Breeding & the Cane Corso: What Should I Consider?

When breeding your Cane Corso, it is good to establish what purpose you are breeding for. What are the traits you want to pass on to future generations? In some cases, breeders may want to breed for coat color and conformation as a primary objective. In this case, it is good to have an understanding of genetics and how it will play out. In this chapter, we will cover the basic steps in breeding your Cane Corso.

When breeding your Cane Corso, it is good to establish why you are breeding and what goals you have.

Selection

Breeding starts with selecting a male and female that complement each other. Choose a pair of dogs that have the traits you find desirable for future generations. Pair up dogs that are about the same in size, as this will help minimize complications during whelping that can arise from overly-large puppies.

Before breeding the two dogs, have a vet perform complete physical examinations on both. Since Cane Corsos are genetically prone to conditions like hip dysplasia, your vet should check both dogs' hips. They should also test for communicable diseases like brucellosis, which can lead to infertility. Make sure that any illnesses have been ruled out before breeding.

Heat Cycles

Observe the female dog closely for signs of a heat cycle or estrus. These include vulvar swelling and darkening in color, as well as the production of discharge that will change from red to clear as the cycle progresses. Cane Corsos, like other larger breeds, come into heat once every 8 to 12 months and are receptive to breeding for about ten days.

Breeding for female Cane Corso's should not be allowed during the first heat cycle, usually at ten to 12 months of age. At this age Cane Corso females are not fully developed in their body and muscle structure, and pregnancy will stunt their growth. The International Cane Corso Federation (ICCF) will not register a litter of pups from a female that was bred before 18 months. Expect a heat cycle to last for about 21 days, and bleeding during the first 11 days.

Pregnancy

For Cane Corsos, the duration of pregnancy is approximately nine weeks. However, there are cases when it takes less than nine weeks before the birth process begins; gestation may also extend for up to a week more. This does not have to be cause for worry: Whether the mother gives birth a bit earlier or later than expected, there is still a high likelihood of healthy puppies being born as long as you are prepared for labor in advance, and can help your Cane Corso give birth.

The development and growth of the fetuses happen at a slow pace until the 4th week of pregnancy. During this period, you will need to provide a special regimen of management and feeding for your Cane Corso bitch, whose susceptibility to infectious diseases is higher at this time.

Have the bitch examined by a vet after the 4th week of pregnancy. Between the 4th and 5th weeks, your vet can already estimate the number of puppies by palpating the dog's abdomen. However, as a safety precaution, you should avoid examining by touch starting from the 5th to 6th week of pregnancy. During the 8th week, the fetuses' heads form, and they may start moving.

From the 4th to 6th week of pregnancy, make sure to feed the dog thrice a day and provide additional amounts of fish and meat food, cottage cheese, milk, and porridge made with milk and soups.

In the second half of the pregnancy, it is advisable to give your Cane Corso bitch pureed raw fruit and vegetables and reduce the quantity of starchy foods.

Birth

When the Cane Corso gives birth, you must remove the slime on the pups so that it doesn't enter their respiratory passages, which can lead to asphyxia.

Be ready with a bandaging thread that you have disinfected in advance. The mother will chew through each pup's umbilical cord; if not, you must tie the thread around the cord about 2 inches below the puppy's belly and then cut it using sterilized scissors. You should then wipe each puppy with a clean, dry towel. The remaining part of the umbilical cord will dry and fall off a few days after birth.

If you observe a puppy breathing heavily, take it, and shake the puppy with its bottom up, while holding its head with your fingers. This will help clear its respiratory passages of the slime that has been obstructing its breathing.

If there are complications during labor, call your vet right away.

After the female Cane Corso has completed giving birth, take her outside for a walk in the open air. You should then clean her genitals with warm water, and then wipe them with a clean, soft cloth.

Litter

The Cane Corso usually gives birth to a litter of 6 to 10 puppies. Expect the puppies to be friendly, inquisitive, and trusting creatures. As you spend time with them, they will move around your feet, get into your lap, nibble on your fingers and toes, and go around trying to inspect everything. Observe the puppies' interactions with each other and look for the unique characteristics of each puppy.

As puppies interact with their littermates, you may already see signs of their temperaments. Try to observe which puppies are dominant, outgoing, and noisy, and which ones are more submissive and quiet. As they play, observe which pup/s tend to grab the toys first and win tugs-of-war, and which pup/s appear physically weaker or more subdued.

What is Unique About the Female Cane Corso's Temperament?

Another point to ask when considering buying a Cane Corso is the sex of the dog. Although it is a point of debate, experts claim that there tend to be differences between male and female dogs.

According to some sources, female dogs are more likely to show changes in their mood: They can be quite affectionate when they feel happy, but show signs of grumpiness when especially if they are not inclined to do something.

Female dogs may sometimes come up to you and "ask" to be petted, and then walk away when they feel they have had enough, as a way of showing their independence. Most female dogs also tend to be less physical than male dogs.

What is Unique About the Male Cane Corso's Temperament?

Speaking very generally about male dogs, they tend to display more stable moods, and they also tend to be more adventurous. However, keep in mind that temperament varies among individual dogs—some females have more aggressive personalities, and some males are more playful or affectionate by nature.

Another thing to consider, especially for owners who are easily embarrassed, is that the genitals of male dogs are quite visible. This may disconcert some owners, especially when dogs become aroused and lick their private parts in public.

What is the Life Expectancy of a Cane Corso?

The life expectancy of a Cane Corso is ten to twelve years.

Your Cane Corso and Old Age

As Cane Corsos mature, both their physical and nutritional needs will change. Their nature and characteristics will undergo changes. Puppies tend to be higher energy, and excitable whereas mature Cane Corsos are sedate and calmer. A Cane Corso is considered to be entering old age when it turns seven years old. By this time, you get to see observable changes in its diet and behavior.

Weight gain is the first noticeable change. Aging Cane Corsos will gain weight around the abdominal area. In some rarer cases, some may also lose weight as they lose the ability to absorb nutrition from food. You will also notice a decrease in activity levels. Your Cane Corso will be less active. They will still go with you for a quick walk or romp, but they are now less likely to self-exercise or run when off the leash, out in the yard.

Older Cane Corsos will now have trouble getting up or down. They may feel stiff when first standing or develop limps. They may also start refusing food or drink more water. Their coat will change and turn gray or white around the muzzle area, and shedding may become more frequent and constant.

Another thing to look for is dental problems. Your Cane Corso may have bouts of bad breath, bleeding or inflamed gums and maybe even tooth loss. This might be less prevalent if your dog had good dental care throughout its life.

The aging Cane Corso will now be more likely to sleep longer. They will sleep more soundly compared to when they were younger. Hearing and vision loss may now occur at this time. However, some Cane Corsos can begin to accept this and still live happy and normal lives. Watching your Cane Corso go through these changes is a sad process, so it's good to make arrangements for your dog, and make their remaining years as happy and as comfortable as it can be.

CHAPTER 14

Showing Your Cane Corso

Y ou are now a proud owner of a Cane Corso, and somehow you want to take it to the next level. You want to show your Cane Corso! Here are some pointers to consider specifically for the Cane Corso breed.

Your Cane Corso's socialization is immensely important to its potential as a show dog.

How Do I Show My Cane Corso?

Put effort into socialization.

Your puppy socialization is immensely important for its potential as a show dog. Perfect conformation is one thing, but if a dog is shy around people, it will have difficulty performing well enough to win in shows. Develop a proud and confident dog. Remember that confidence is a key trait found in all top show dogs that judges love to see.

You can develop this by doing the following:

- Taking your dog with you everywhere you go.
- Exposing your dog to unfamiliar people, places, noises, and situations.
- Taking your dog to puppy socialization classes in which it will get accustomed to interacting with many other dogs.
- Encouraging people to pet your dog and look gently in its mouth, so that your dog becomes comfortable with having strangers (including judges, eventually) touch them.

Do bring your dog to conformation training classes.

Such classes are offered by many kennel clubs. If you are a novice exhibitor, this will be a valuable experience because the instructors will be experienced dog handlers who can teach you all of the basics of presenting a dog in the ring. At the same time, your dog will learn how it is expected to behave when competing at a dog show.

Instructors will teach you important skills, such as gaiting your dog around the ring. Plus, instructors and other breeders attending the class can take a look at your dog, check its conformation, and provide advice on whether it is fit for the show ring. As a novice exhibitor, it may difficult to accept, but it is sometimes a reality that your dog does not have what it takes to win. Learning this early on can help save considerable money.

Remember that clean dogs are always appreciated by judges.

On the one hand, excessive grooming is not encouraged for some breeds because it can change the dog's coat from its proper texture. However, no judge would like to touch an unclean dog. It may not be necessary to bathe your dog weekly to maintain its proper texture, but you can spot clean areas like the face, legs, and undercarriage. Depending on your dog's bath schedule, you may want to bathe your dog a day before the show weekend, and then provide brushing and spot bathing as needed to maintain its optimal condition.

Position your dog in the middle of the lineup.

As you enter the ring, avoid being the first or last dog in the lineup if you can. Judges sometimes have competitors line up in the order presented in the show catalog; but if this is not the case, try to go somewhere in the middle. This will allow you a little more time to get your dog stacked in perfect position, whereas if you are first in line, the judge will examine your dog first as soon as the entire group is gaited around the show ring. Meanwhile, the last handler also has to work quickly, because as soon as their dog completes its turn around the ring, the judge will give all the competitors one final look. Being in the middle will give you enough time to maintain your dog's appearance before the judge runs the whole group around the ring for one final time and decides on the winner.

Always be aware of the judge's actions.

Keep an eye on the judge, so you know where they are standing in the ring and what they are doing at all times. This way, you can ensure that the judge will never notice your dog standing incorrectly and revealing weaknesses.

Also, your attention to the judge will help you appear more professional. Since each dog is only allotted approximately two minutes for judging, you do not want to waste the judge's time calling you twice if you are not paying attention.

Practice gaiting your dog at the right speed.

Most show dogs do have their minor faults somewhere. Observe your dog. See if there is a fault in its gait, and then figure out how slow or fast you should walk so your dog moves at its best. You can ask a friend to walk your dog for you, as you observe.

Position your dog between you and the judge at all times.

Remember that the judge is there to evaluate your dog, not you. Your dog should be between the two of you all throughout the competition. If you are told to walk your dog in the "L" pattern, switch hands with the lead and walk with your dog on the other side of you so that your legs do not obstruct the judge's view of your dog.

Finally, stay calm.

You've finally made it! Your emotional state and demeanor can make or break your dog's performance. Your dog can sense through your hands and the lead if you are feeling nervous and stressed, and this will likely affect its confidence. Take it easy and focus on what's happening in the ring. If you and your dog are adequately prepared, you should have no reason to feel anxious. At the end of the day, it is the judge who will decide on the winner—something you can never fully control. Focus on what you've rehearsed and work with your dog as a team.

The Italian Kennel Club

The Italian Kennel Club, also known as the "Ente Nazionale della Cinofilia Italiana" (ENCI), is the organization that is primarily responsible for the standards and business related to dog pedigrees in Italy.

Originally formed in 1882, ENCI is a full member of the Fédération Cynologique Internationale, the world canine organization. While its main office is in Milan, the club has regional offices in various locations in Italy. The organization provides judging for dog shows as well as other related services.

In 2009, the club organized about 400 dog shows, and its stud books included more than 150,000 listed dogs. Note that ENCI pays particular attention to breeds that are recognized as having originated in Italy, including the Cane Corso.

CHAPTER 15

What are the Controversies Surrounding the Cane Corso Breed?

C ane Corsos are often used for dog fighting and this is one of the reasons they have a reputation as an aggressive breed. In dog fighting, two dogs are placed in a fighting pit and forced to fight each other violently for the entertainment and benefit of spectator-gamblers.

Cane Corsos are often used for dog fighting, this is one of the reasons they have a reputation as an aggressive breed, but that is mostly down to environment.

Cane Corso and Illegal Dog Fighting

Dogs are, by nature, very social animals. It cannot be repeated often enough that aggression is a trait that is developed in some dogs due to irresponsible handling. Humans who use dogs for fighting keep them chained, taunt, and even starve them to elicit extreme instincts for survival and instigate aggression.

Is the Cane Corso an Aggressive Breed?

There is a purpose why a breed is developed, and potential owners should always research why their desired breed was developed to determine whether it fits your needs and lifestyle. For example, Australian Shepherds were bred to herd, while Labrador retrievers were bred for hunting. Cane Corsos were originally bred as guard dogs as well as to hunt strong creatures like a wild boar.

Because of the traits that were selected in the breed, Cane Corsos have a strong instinct to protect their people from strangers—basically, anyone who is not part of the family circle. Thus, Cane Corsos are usually not particularly friendly to strangers and often do not like other dogs or pets. For these reasons, Cane Corsos are best suited to experienced handlers. If you plan to get a Cane Corso, educate your household about these large dogs' characteristics and ensure that everyone in your family is comfortable with them.

It is always good to have an ounce of prevention before anything else, so if you are getting a puppy, get one from a reliable breeder and make sure you meet its parents to get an idea of their temperament. The Cane Corso is strong willed, and it's good to enroll it in obedience training from as early as puppyhood. A Cane Corso must be taught to obey you.

There are many types and reasons for aggression in dogs, one of which is dominance aggression. An example of this would be a dog growling or snapping when a person gets near things that the dog considers its "possessions," like food or a toy. It is important to teach your Cane Corso never to cross the line between appropriate and inappropriate behavior such as this. As your dog's "pack leader," show your dog that you are in control—Cane Corsos tend to form very close bonds with their owners, and you should establish their obedience as part of that bond.

A form of canine aggression that tends to happen between two males is a dog going after another dog. The likelihood of such behaviors is decreased by having your dog neutered. Whenever you encounter another dog while you are walking your Cane Corso, stay in control of your dog at all times, and give praise or treats if your dog ignores the other.

Cane Corsos tend to be very territorial, so it may be more difficult to handle situations when other dogs are on or near your property. Again, assert your role as the "leader" and gently but firmly show your dog what is considered acceptable behavior and what is not. Cane Corsos respond well to positive reinforcement, so make use of praise and treats.

What Can I Do to Ensure a Good Experience?

Cane Corsos tend to be very territorial, so you may need to handle with care situations when other dogs are on or near your property.

To ensure a good experience, it is good to know the developmental stages of a Cane Corso and what happens during this period and what you should do in these stages.

From 0 to 7 weeks, the puppy is in the Neonatal, Transition, Awareness, and Canine Socialization Period. During this time, the puppy is always with its mother and littermates. Puppies at this stage are learning crucial information about social interaction, play, and inhibiting aggression.

This is a critical period for puppies, so it is imperative that they stay with their mother and littermates. This is the time when puppies first learn the most important lesson of all: accepting discipline.

From 8 to 11 weeks of age, puppies are in the Fear Imprint Period. During this time, you should avoid scaring the puppy. If a puppy has a painful or frightening experience during this time, the effect on the puppy will last longer than if it had happened at any other time in its life.

From 13 to 16 weeks, puppies are in their seniority classification period—also known as the "age of cutting." Puppies at this stage are cutting teeth and also start determining who the pack leader is. At about 4.5 months, puppies lose their milk teeth, and their adult teeth grow in. At this point, the puppy will start serious chewing. Dog's teeth do not set in their jaws until they are between 6 to 10 months old—before that, puppies will feel a physical need to exercise their mouths by chewing. Discourage any biting at this stage—biting is a sign of dominance, and you need to establish that you are a strong and persistent leader.

This is also the time to start formal training, as this will help you further establish your leadership. If a puppy bites you, mimic the way its mother would teach it not to bite by giving a quick pinch to its lip while staring it in the eye and reacting loudly in its face.

Between 4 to 8 months, puppies are in the Play Instinct Period and Flight Instinct Period. Puppies may show a tendency to wander off and ignore their owner. During this time, keep your puppy on a leash and continue training it. Your handling of the puppy at this stage strongly influences whether the puppy will come to you when you call it.

Between 6 to 14 months, puppies go through their second Fear Imprint Period or Fear of New Situations Period. Your dog may exhibit fear when in unfamiliar situations, and even in familiar ones. They may hesitate to go near new people or things. During such instances, just be patient and act in a matter of fact way. Do not ever force the dog to face the situation it fears. At the same time, avoid petting the scared puppy or talking to it in a soothing voice, as the puppy will most likely interpret these behaviors as praise for being scared.

If you have the intention of neutering or spaying the dog, do it in this period.

From one to four years, dogs are in their Maturity Period. From time to time, your dog may exhibit increased aggression or resume testing for dominance. It is important that you continue to train your mature dog.

Conclusion

A Cane Corso is a large and magnificent looking breed of dog with an illustrative history, and loyal demeanor honed through time. It is a dog with a long and tested history of being a protective and loyal guard dog. Bringing home one means you're going to have a friend and protector for its entire lifespan. In this book, we have discussed how the Corso matches up to other breeds, and it is certainly not a lightweight.

The Corso is one of the most intelligent and highly trainable dogs out there!

The Cane Corso delivers where other breeds may not. It thrives on physical activity as well as mental stimulation. It would welcome obedience training classes to unlock its full potential. The Cane Corso can grow to be a very disciplined companion, unlike other dogs. It has a staid and serious character that can allow you to relax but know you have a secure protector.

If you want a serious dog that has more than just cuteness or goofiness, the Cane Corso is for you. Beware though, the Cane Corso is a serious investment. You have to train it thoroughly so that it won't develop bad habits. It's a large dog and can be tough to handle. Bring home a Cane Corso and embrace the necessary responsibilities that go with it, and you would have a loyal dog for life.

Who knows, your Cane Corso may just save your life one day. Enjoy the Journey with your Cane Corso, and I hope you create many lasting memories together with this wonderful breed!

Cane Corso Trusted Resource List

Breeders of Cane Corso (USA)

- **About Time Cane Corso Italiano**
  http://www.abouttimecanecorso.com/
  USA Breeder, New Mexico based

- **Black Pearl Cane Corso**
  https://www.blackpearlcanecorso.com/
  USA Breeder, Michigan based, breeds for health and temperament

- **Mad River Cane Corso**
  http://www.madrivercanecorso.com/
  USA Breeder, Ohio based, breeds dogs with stable temperament

- **Shipley Cane Corso**
  http://www.shipleycanecorso.com/
  USA Breeder, Ohio based, breeds for stable temperament

Breeders of Cane Corso (Canada)

- **Capital Cane Corso**
  http://www.capitalcanecorso.com/
  Canada Breeder, Ottawa, dogs are ICCF and AKC certified

Breeders of Cane Corso (Europe)

- **Boleyn Cane Corso**
  http://www.canecorso.me.uk/
  UK Trusted Long Time Cane Corso Breeder, Family Run.

- **Spunk Gang**
  http://www.spunkgang.com/
  Serbian Breeder, breeds for quality

Breeders of Cane Corso (Australia and New Zealand)

- **Corsarii New Zealand Kennel**
  http://www.canecorso.co.nz/
  New Zealand Breeder, can ship puppies

Cane Corso Rescue

- **Cane Corso Rescue, Inc.**
  https://canecorsorescue.org/
  shelter for dogs, gives up Cane Corsos for adoption

Made in the USA
Las Vegas, NV
31 March 2022